SURvIVING
A SCHOOL
SHOOTING

Be Safe

Loren Antenore

SURVIVING A SCHOOL SHOOTING

A Plan of Action for Parents, Teachers, and Students

Loren W. Christensen
Foreword by Lt. Col. Dave Grossman

Paladin Press • Boulder, Colorado

Also by Loren W. Christensen:
Anything Goes: Practical Karate for the Streets
Deadly Force Encounters: What Cops Need to Know to Mentally and Physically Prepare
 for and Survive a Gunfight (with Dr. Alexis Artwohl)
Extreme Joint Locking and Breaking: Restraint and Submission Techniques for the Street
Far Beyond Defensive Tactics: Advanced Concepts, Techniques, Drills, and Tricks
 for Cops on the Street
Fighting Dirty: A "No Sweat" Guide to Hardcore Self-Defense Training (DVD)
Fighting Power: How to Develop Explosive Punches, Kicks, Blocks, and Grappling
Gangbangers: Understanding the Deadly Minds of America's Street Gangs
On Combat: The Psychology and Physiology of Deadly Combat in War and in Peace
 (by Lt. Col. Dave Grossman with Loren W. Christensen)
Restraint and Control Strategies: State-of-the-Art Defensive Tactics for Law Enforcement
 and Security Professionals (DVD)
Skid Row Beat: A Street Cop's Walk on the Wild Side
Speed Training: How to Develop Your Maximum Speed for Martial Arts
Speed Training: The Video: Developing Maximum Speed in Martial Arts Training (DVD)
Surviving Workplace Violence: What to Do Before a Violent Incident;
 What to Do When the Violence Explodes
Warriors: On Living with Courage, Discipline, and Honor
The Way Alone: Your Path to Excellence in the Martial Arts

Surviving a School Shooting: A Plan of Action for Parents, Teachers, and Students
by Loren W. Christensen

Copyright © 2008 by Loren W. Christensen

ISBN 13: 978-1-58160-659-1
Printed in the United States of America

Published by Paladin Press, a division of
Paladin Enterprises, Inc.
Gunbarrel Tech Center
7077 Winchester Circle
Boulder, Colorado 80301 USA
+1.303.443.7250

Direct inquiries and/or orders to the above address.

PALADIN, PALADIN PRESS, and the "horse head" design are trademarks belonging to
Paladin Enterprises and registered in United States Patent and Trademark Office.

Neither the author nor the publisher assumes any responsibility for the use or misuse of
information contained in this book.

Visit our website at www.paladin-press.com

Table of Contents

Acknowledgments

A crushing hug to Lisa, my significant other, who is always there for me, and always so supportive when I begin to burn out and get cranky at the end of a writing project. Gassho.

Big thanks to Amy and Jace Widmer, my daughter and son-in-law, for reading the first draft, giving corrections and offering wonderful input. Both are schoolteachers of remarkable patience, skill, and compassion. Every parent can only hope that their kids learn from teachers of this caliber.

Thanks to my friend and mentor Lt. Col. Dave Grossman for writing the Foreword. I encourage every parent and teacher to get a copy of his book *Stop Teaching Our Kids to Kill*.

Thanks to my friend, Stephanie Solomon-Lopez, a Senior Dispatcher at the Bureau of Emergency Communications in Portland Oregon for fine-tuning exactly what information 9-1-1 needs to respond quickly and appropriately to a school shooting.

A deep bow to Kathy Wirtes, a Paladin Press editor extraordinaire, for her care and attention to detail.

Many thanks to those teachers and other experts who took the time to e-mail me about their experiences, but whose names and e-mails were lost irretrievably when my computer crashed not once, but twice during the course of writing this book.

Columbine 9-1-1 From the Library

April 20, 1999

Peggy: *Yes, I'm a teacher at Columbine High School and there is a student here with a gun. He just shot out a window. I believe, um, I'm at Columbine High School. I don't know what's in my shoulder. If it was just some glass. I don't know what's going on.*

Dispatcher: *Has anyone been injured, ma'am?*

Peggy: *I am, yes! And the school is in a panic and I'm in the library. I've got students down. Kids under the table! My kids are screaming, under the table, kids, and my teachers are trying to take control of things. We need police here.*

Dispatcher: *OK, OK, we're getting them. Who is the student, ma'am?*

Peggy: *I don't know who the student is. I saw a student outside . . . I said what was going on out there. (Talking to students) I don't think that's a really good idea. (Back to dispatcher) And we were waiting to see what was going on. He turned the gun straight at us and shot and my God, the window went out and the kid standing there with me, I think he got hit.*

Dispatcher: *OK, we got help on the way, ma'am.*

Peggy: *Oh God! Oh God! Kids, just stay down. Do we know where he's at? I'm in the library. He's upstairs. He's right outside of here. He's outside this hall. There are lines of people . . . Kids, just stay down! Do we know where he's at? He's outside in the hall. There's alarms and things going off and smoke. (Yelling): My God, smoke is coming into this room. I've got the kids under a table. I don't know what's happening in the rest of the building. Shouldn't someone else be calling 9-1-1?*

Dispatcher: *Yes, we have a lot of people on. I need you to stay on the line with me. We need to know what's going on.*

Peggy: *I am on the floor.*

Dispatcher: *You've got the kids there?*

Peggy: *I've got every student in this library on the floor. (Yelling): You guys just stay on the floor!*

Dispatcher: *Is there any way you can lock the doors?*

Peggy: *Um, smoke is coming in from out there and I'm a little . . . My God, it's . . . (Bang! Bang! Bang! Bang! Bang! Bang!) My God, the gun is right outside my door. OK, I don't think I'm going to go out there. We're not going to go to the door. I've got the kids on the floor. I got all of the kids in the library on the floor.*

The two shooters, who had already shot several people else-where on the campus, did enter the library. They taunted, shot, and killed 10 more students, wounded another dozen, and shot at several others. They then left to shoot at more people in other rooms, throw a pipe bomb, and taunt more terrorized students. They eventually returned to the library where they would shoot themselves to death.

When it was all over, Eric Harris and Dylan Klebold had murdered 12 students and one teacher at Columbine High School.

Foreword

In 2004, 48 children were murdered in U.S. schools and more than a hundred thousand were seriously injured in incidents of school violence. Meanwhile, it has been many years since a single child has been killed or injured by school fire. Every school has sprinklers, alarms, drills, and extinguishers, but why aren't we preparing for the thing that is killing our kids?

Law enforcement agencies and school districts need to have in place contingency plans for school shootings—and they must practice them. Although we are thinking primarily about school shootings, these contingency plans should also apply to mass murders and active shooters in other large areas (hospitals, malls, workplaces, sporting events, churches, etc.). In particular, we have to recognize that a model of one plan is the "active shooter," a term that police agencies define as a suspect or suspects whose "activity is causing death and serious bodily injury now."

ASK LOCAL LAW ENFORCEMENT
TO INSPECT YOUR CAMPUS

While you might want the police, in particular SWAT, to discreetly inspect your campus, there can be value in having them do it during school hours. The kids will see them and it will deter many potential killers. (Some people think that a uniform presence will raise the fear level, others say there is already a very high fear level.) You probably don't want SWAT dressed in their full call-out gear; their regular uniform is fine. If the school administration doesn't agree that there is positive value to doing this, you might have to compromise to just a few officers, say three teams of two in regular uniform, evaluating and becoming familiar with the layout of the school.

Officers should spend an entire day at the school. They should discuss and observe such things as possible approach routes, and assembly areas where buses and parents drop off kids in the morning, which is when the Pearl High School shooting occurred in Mississippi. They should evaluate lunchtime when kids are in the cafeteria, which is when the shootings happened in Springfield, Oregon, and at Columbine in Colorado, and they should discuss and observe end-of-the-day traffic congestion, a place and condition that offers a target-rich environment.

Officers should look at a school assembly in the auditorium and discuss how they would approach a shooting in that populated space. They should evaluate roofs to consider dealing with a shooter firing down at students (as occurred at the University of Texas in 1966 when former Marine Charles Whitman killed 16 people from a tower on the campus). They should even consider the possibility of a shooting or bombing at a school sporting event. I am surprised we have not seen this yet, especially as much as the profile of the average shooter is such a "jock-hater."

All contingency plans should incorporate the fire department's preplanned response to the school, especially since they already know the location of utility panels, ductwork, and conduits. They usually have building blueprints in their preplan package (something very important for any SWAT response). Inspecting officers should know about any video surveillance security system and from where it's monitored.

It's critical to incorporate the school resource officer (SRO) in the evaluation and planning since he knows the layout of the school. The SRO is probably familiar with potential troublemakers, and he knows most of the student leaders and the official and unofficial opinion shapers within student groups and cliques. The police will already have profiles on students who have had run-ins with the law, particularly in small to midsize towns. That information should be included in all contingency packages.

The kind of plans officers devise—such as how to evacuate kids, secure the inner and outer perimeter, set up an officer sniper, employ rapid entry while shots are firing, and how to deal with bombs—apply to daycare centers and churches too, which, sadly, have increasingly been targets.

CREATE A PLAN FOR LOCKDOWNS

Preparing Kids for an Incident

Any school that does not have a lockdown drill is negligent and liable.

When an active shooter is in the school, kids should get out quickly or, according to teachers' guidance, lock themselves into rooms and barricade the doors. School killers are seldom out to take hostages. Most are on a spree, out to kill as many people as possible; "take no prisoners" could well be their motto.

When SWAT teams or other officers enter, their orders to students and staff should be, "Hit the deck and stay down until told otherwise."

Preparing Teachers and Staff

Preparing and drilling teachers and staff is at the heart of the operation. This can be done like a fire plan, which should be the model for planning and preparation for a school shooting. Each classroom needs assessment by the police, just as each classroom needs a separate fire plan. While some rooms might be perfect for securing students behind locked and barricaded doors, other locations won't be, such as what happened when students hid in the library at Columbine High. When a room isn't secure, drills must include moving people to a better room. It doesn't have to be Fort Knox; it just needs to slow down a shooter long enough for the police to respond.

Important: Part of the drill should include teachers dialing the phone number to report emergencies. Most classroom phones require dialing a number(s) to get an outside line before dialing 9-1-1. This must be rehearsed so it can be done under great stress.

CREATE A PLAN FOR EVACUATIONS

Any school that does not have an evacuation plan and periodically practice that plan is morally negligent and legally liable. Since there is one in place for fire and bomb drills, it's easy to add another, which must include a signal for its execution. Periodic fire drills are a must and evacuation in response to a real fire is a must. Evacuating in response to a bomb scare, however, is a judgment call.

Do not evacuate into parking lots! The easiest most deadly kind of bomb to manufacture and transport is a car bomb. Some mini-Timothy McVeigh could build one with a propane tank or, even worse, 400 pounds of primed fertilizer. Hidden in his car, it could be ignited with a remote device. If kids must evacuate into a parking lot, make it the faculty parking lot and then rigidly control access to that lot. (Consistently and immediately tow all unauthorized cars.) When teachers evacuate kids to the lawn or faculty parking lot, look for anything that doesn't belong there: a box, bag, pipe, or freshly upturned dirt—and stay away from those objects.

In every case, the killer is looking for a "soft" target, a military term meaning an easy target so he can make a statement by killing as many innocents as possible. He knows that he won't get on the news if he doesn't have a high body count. If we can "harden" the target, that is, make it difficult for him to shoot people, it will deter many potential killers. Case in point: The shooter in the LA Jewish daycare center in 1999 looked at two other hard sites before he found one without security.

CONCLUSION

All of these measures are vital to save lives and deter these tragic crimes. This book is a treasure trove of wisdom and advice that will help us prepare for school violence in the same way that the fire department helps us to prepare for school fire.

There is nothing more important than our children and our grandchildren. They are our greatest treasure and our hope for the future. Every child is infinitely precious to someone, and therefore each child must be infinitely precious to us all. Thus, the security and safety of our children is the most important function that any society can perform.

Today these precious little ones are threatened from within and from without to a degree greater than ever before in living memory. Those who would do us harm—from both inside and outside our borders—know that the path toward the greatest notoriety, and the way to bring the severest suffering to us and to our collective body, is to attack our children.

Thus, this book is a vital resource to anyone who is concerned about the safety and well-being of our children. Hopefully, everyone falls into that category! So don't just read this book, but study it and apply it so that our little ones, our future, can live and prosper in the years to come.

Dave Grossman
Lt. Col. U.S. Army (Ret.)
Author of *On Killing, On Combat,* and
Stop Teaching Our Kids to Kill
www.killology.com

Introduction

There was nothing in the air at Virginia Tech on April 16, 2007, to indicate that before lunch a crazed gunman would fire 170 rounds from two semi-automatic handguns to slaughter 32 people, wound at least 17, and send a bone-chilling dread through a university, a community, and a country before finally killing himself.

That was Monday, the beginning of a long week.

On Tuesday, bomb threats and reports of armed men forced universities in Oklahoma, Tennessee, and Texas to lock down as uniformed police officers and bomb squads roared to the campuses to search and try to restore a sense of normalcy.

On Wednesday, officers returned to the university president's office at Virginia Tech to investigate suspicious activity. It was a false alarm, and it wasn't the only one that day. There were threats, false alarms, and legitimate gun and bomb incidents on campuses across the country.

On Thursday, police arrested a teen near Seattle for carrying three loaded guns and extra ammunition. Another in Huntersville, North Carolina, shot and killed himself after pointing a pistol at students in a high school parking lot. In the small community of Riverton, Kansas, five teens were arrested after leaving a threatening message on Myspace.com. In the bedroom of one suspect, deputies found guns, ammunition, knives, and coded messages. In their school lockers, police found material about Armageddon and documents about firearms. Their plan was to wear black trench coats, disable the school's security camera system, and then attack all-out; they had been planning it for months.

On Friday, the Tenafly, New Jersey, school district closed after receiving information of a bomb threat, threats to use an AK-47 assault rifle, and threats to use poison. The one making the threats turned out not to be a teen student but rather a 28-year-old man, a hardcore meth user. "I'll make Cho look mild," he promised chillingly, refering to the Virgina Tech killer. In another incident, entire California school districts in Yuba and Sutter counties closed after receiving bomb threats. The same happened at the University of Tennessee after someone threatened them. Then a small bomb exploded outside a high school in Parker, Colorado, and authorities apprehended a suspect carrying a second explosive device.

While these events are always in greater number after a major school shooting, there are similar ones, to a lesser degree, every day in our schools. Campuses are a hunting ground for psychotics. Our campuses are, to use a military term, a target-rich environment for the mentally ill and for extremists looking for multiple targets, multiple kills.

By the time most children enter school, they are aware of violence in the world, in particular, that there are school shootings and bomb threats. They have heard their parents and older siblings talk about it, they have seen it in movies, in the news, in magazines, and on television. How children respond to these events depends on their temperament, maturity, experience with violence, and the manner in which the events are presented to them. Modern schools are not the same ones we went to. Today there is extraordinary violence, sex crimes, drugs, guns, knives, bombs, gangs, shootings, killings, robberies, and even violent parents.

There is one major component that not only allows these things to happen but prevents anything being done about it: denial. Denial from school officials and denial from parents. When those in a position of influence put on rose-tinted glasses and say stubbornly, "It can't happen at this school," or deny or downplay the significance of an event, it opens the door for the situation to worsen.

Kids want to feel safe and secure, even those teens whose tough exterior attitude would suggest otherwise. It's the task of the parents and the school to provide that sense of safety. Students also need to know that when they are afraid of something or someone that there is a person they can go to, a person who will listen and take action.

Within the pages of this book are ideas and techniques to help teach parents how to talk to their kids about what is going on in school and how to listen to what kids are saying. Kids of all ages will learn how to feel safer at school and how to inform an adult when they hear about someone making threats or when they see something dangerous. Everyone will learn about lockdown and evacuation procedures, how to think ahead about how they would respond to a shooting, and what to do when a shooting occurs: when to run and how to run; when to hide and how to hide; when to fight and how to fight.

This book presents ideas about how you can work with school administrators and local law enforcement to ensure that they are doing all that they can to keep our schools safe.

You won't find denial within these pages but rather truth and honesty about a horrific event that *most assuredly* will happen again.

<table>
<tr><td>

Chapter

1

</td><td>

The Threat

</td></tr>
</table>

There's another Jeff Weise out there somewhere, maybe in your school. Look for him.

—Karla Lajeunesse, whose daughter, Ashley, survived after being shot by gunman Jeffrey Weise in 2005 at Minnesota's Red Lake High School[1]

Most adults experienced a different school environment than what exists today. When I was in high school, we acted out by hanging a kid's underwear from a flagpole, rebelled by slamming our books on the floor in study hall to protest the teacher's unreasonable insistence that we actually study, and settled our differences by fist fighting behind the gymnasium.

Times have changed. Today, kids act out, rebel, and settle their differences by bringing guns, knives, and bombs to school. As a Portland (Oregon) Police Gang Enforcement Officer, I responded to countless cases of weapons in schools, drive-by shootings, and brutal gang fights. For example, I investigated a case in which a teen didn't like a look another kid had given him when passing in the hall. The offended boy left the school, went to a nearby market, bought a machete, returned to the school, and hacked a large wedge out of the other boy's shoulder. He was probably aiming for the kid's neck but missed. While no doubt there have always been incidents of extreme violence in schools, the difference today is that it's abundant. Violence is extreme and more and more commonplace.

Commonplace. What an ugly word to use in a sentence about violence in a place where our kids spend their day. But incidents involving firearms in schools occur weekly somewhere in this country, so often that such incidents now get minimum media coverage, if at all.

One type of campus shooting that isn't commonplace, although it no longer surprises us the same way it did in the late 1990s, is the school massacre. The shooter—usually a student, though some have been adults—brings an arsenal to school where, to use a descriptive military term, there exists a target-rich environment. Then the shooter has a field day.

While such an event might not surprise us as it once did, it still shocks. It shocks us because of where it occurs and because of the sheer randomness of how the shooter slaughters his victims. Its horrific devastation instills terror into the hearts of those kids and adults on the scene and on the rest of us who see it on the news and wonder: Could it happen in my community? Could it happen where my children go to school?

The answer is—yes.

RECENT SCHOOL SHOOTINGS

Lake Worth, Florida, May 26, 2000—a 13-year-old killed his teacher on the last day of classes after he was told he couldn't speak to two girls in the class.

Red Lion, Pennsylvania, April 24, 2003—in a crowded junior high school cafeteria, a 14-year-old boy shot and killed the principal and then shot himself to death.

Red Lake Indian Reservation, Minnesota, March 21, 2005—a teenager walked into a high school and shot dead five students, a teacher, and an unarmed guard. Before he left for school that morning, he killed his grandfather and his grandfather's girlfriend.

Essex, Vermont, Aug. 24, 2006—a 26-year-old man entered an elementary school in search of his ex-girlfriend. When he couldn't find her, he killed one teacher and wounded a second one. He tried to kill himself with two shots into his head, but he survived and was arrested.

Bailey, Colorado, Sept. 27, 2006—a 53-year-old drifter took seven girls hostage at Platte Canyon High School, sexually assaulted them, and used them as human shields. Several hours later, he killed one girl and then himself.

Cazenovia, Wisconsin, Sept. 29, 2006—a 15-year-old brought two guns to a rural school and killed the principal who, the day prior, had disciplined him for possessing tobacco on school property.

Nickel Mines, Pennsylvania, Oct. 2, 2006—a 32-year-old gunman took hostages in a West Nickel Mines Amish schoolhouse and killed five students and then himself.

Blacksburg, Virginia, April 16, 2007—a 23-year-old Virginia Tech student shot at least 50 people on the University campus, killing 32 of them before killing himself in the deadliest school shooting in modern U.S. history.

DeKalb, Illinois, Feb. 14, 2008—A 27-year-old former student opens fire at Northern Illinois University, killing five and injuring 16 before killing himself.

The Justice Department reports show that every day in the United States, more than 100,000 kids bring firearms and knives to school in their pockets, backpacks, and inside waistbands.

Were these violent incidents the only ones that happened in U.S. schools since 2000? Hardly. They simply represent shootings that were given intense media attention probably because they happened within school buildings. But there are countless others—a few noted below—that occur every year on or near school property that are not only deadly but have the potential to be far worse.

Columbus, Georgia, Aug. 14, 2003—Several middle school kids went into the woods behind the school to watch a fight. One of the boys pulled a handgun and fatally shot a 14-year-old high school girl who was visiting one of her former teachers.

San Diego, California, Sept. 4, 2003—a teenager jogging with his cross-country team was shot and killed when his own father ambushed him. The father subsequently killed himself after a standoff with the police.

Hopkinsville, Kentucky, Sept. 16, 2003—a 16-year-old girl shot and killed another teen and then killed herself while both sat in a car across the street from her school.

Porter, Oklahoma, Dec. 8, 2003—while riding on a school bus, one teen stabbed another to death and then jumped out the rear door.

Henderson, Nevada, Jan. 21, 2004—a 40-year-old man shot a hostage he had been holding in his car and then walked through an elementary school looking for his ex-girlfriend. The police shot and killed him outside the school doors.

Las Vegas, Nevada, Dec. 11, 2007—Six students were shot as they stepped off a school bus on a sunny day in mid-afternoon.

Similar incidents could literally fill this book and perhaps a second. What they all share is an act of violence near a school student body, that target-rich environment that makes us shudder at what could have happened if the already deadly situation had gone just a little differently; if it hadn't ended quite so soon.

Whether we are examining high-profile shootings or the relatively lesser-known ones, it gives us pause that we no longer can consider our kids' schools as safe havens but rather places that are frighteningly vulnerable. The honeymoon is over. We know now that it's not only disgruntled and mentally ill students who pack arsenals to school with bloody mayhem on their minds, but adults, too. We also know that gunfire can erupt anywhere—in the classroom, the hall, the cafeteria, and on the grounds

TRIGGERS

It would seem logical that if we understood the triggers—that thing or things that sets a shooter into motion—we could then eliminate them and thus eliminate the next deadly school mas-

Parental Denial

Too often, parents of violent kids are either indifferent or in denial as to what their kids are doing, and many are simply oblivious to what they are doing. Even worse is when they think their kid's actions are just fine. Consider an 11-year-old boy who wrote notes about his wish to harm others and to see what it would be like to watch them die. He already had some experience killing small animals in a microwave. Inexplicably, several people had reported seeing him roll in manure that was piled behind the school.

When a school psychologist showed the boy's parents his writing and told them what he had been doing, they felt that the lad was just being creative and that he would probably grow up to write screenplays.

sacre. But we don't always know and, even if we did, there is no way to tell how intensely a trigger will be perceived by a disturbed individual. It can ignite sudden violence or set into motion a process within someone that can take hours, days, or weeks to unfold before it manifests into violence.

In most people, however, time and additional experiences dull the intensity of the emotion and any thoughts of mayhem dissipate or simply play out in one's fantasy. For a small number of others, the trigger, coupled with the effects of alcohol or drugs, can expedite and intensify the ripening process. So can another significant negative event, or trigger, such as trauma at home, ridicule from yet another person or persons, or an ugly end to a romantic relationship.

Common Triggers

While a trigger isn't always easy to identify, the following list contains a few common ones:

- Being a victim of bullying or teasing
- Losing a boyfriend or girlfriend
- Hearing about a high-profile school shooting
- Being punished or scolded by a school authority

Mental Health Issues in College

Statistics show that more and more college students are seeking help for mental health problems. Nearly half complain that they have been depressed to the extent they can't function, about a third feel overwhelmed at any given moment, and one out of 10 admits that they have considered suicide.

Parents and teachers should never hesitate to call the authorities should they think a student's mental health has deteriorated to the extent that they might hurt themselves or others.

- Feeling alienated
- Being criticized, mocked, or taunted by other students

Sometimes evidence found on the shooter's person, or in his backpack, school locker, home, or computer reveals possible triggers; other times we simply don't know why he went over the edge. In some cases, we try to employ rational thinking about a shooter's irrational decision. Kip Kinkle, for example, said he believed that the government had planted chips in his head, and he stored explosives under his house because he wanted to prepare for an invasion of Chinese people. He blamed voices in his head that ordered him to kill his parents and then go on a murderous spree at Thurston High School in Springfield, Oregon, on May 20, 1998. Earlier that day he'd been expelled for being in possession of a handgun.

PROFILE OF A SCHOOL SHOOTER

Of course, we want to establish a profile in hopes of finding an easy solution to the problem, but as writer H.L. Mencken once wrote: "For every problem there is a solution which is simple, neat, *and wrong*." The problem that has plagued psychologists and other experts, such as the Secret Service, is that there is little to go on to formulate a viable profile. "Profile?" one expert said. "There isn't one."

We do know that about 90 percent of the shooters had brought a gun to school previously and that an even greater percentage had an infatuation with media violence—movies, TV, and video games. However, as mentioned elsewhere in this chapter and in keeping with Mencken's aphorism, more than 100,000 kids bring guns and knives to school every year, and a vast number of young people are fascinated with media violence.

Stereotypes?

Some experts consider the following a list of stereotypes since it presents profiles that are true for some shooters, but not for all:

- Some are lonely and lack good relationships with friends and family
- Some feel rejected and bullied by others
- Some are fascinated with firearms and explosives
- Some are insecure
- Some have fantasies of grandeur
- Some suffer from mental problems, including depression
- Some try to boost their lack of social skills and influence by bragging that they are going to commit violence on someone or several people
- Some want a sense that they have ultimate control over people and they want others to recognize it

Important: Notice the liberal sprinkling of "some" to describe the above characteristics. It's used for the simple and problematic fact that not all of these characteristics fit the known shooters while many, many other students share these traits but don't gun down their peers and teachers.

In 2002, The United States Secret Service and the United States Department of Education released a report titled "The Final Report and Findings of the Safe School Initiative: Implications for the Prevention of School Attacks in the United States." It runs for 63 pages; to sum it up: *There is no useful profile of a school shooter.* The report included the following descriptions of attackers:

- They were 11 to 21 years old.
- They were 75 percent white. The rest were Hispanic, African American, Native Alaskan, Native American, and Asian.
- They were from happy families, neglectful families, and foster homes. Nearly three-quarters came from two-parent

homes. Only 5 percent came from foster homes or a legal guardian situation.

- They were doing well in school, with 41 percent getting As and Bs. Only 5 percent were failing.
- They revealed no pronounced change in their schoolwork, relationships with friends, interest in school, or disciplinary problems prior to their attacks. A few of them actually showed improvements in their studies prior to the event.
- More than half showed an interest in violence as shown in movies, video games, books, and other media. More than 25 percent were interested in violent movies, another 25 percent liked violent books, 12 percent were interested in violent video games, and 37 percent were interested in their own violent essays, poems, and journal writings.

Middle and high school teachers, who have a different group of students every period, might not be familiar enough with individuals to identify overt indicators. However, they might get clues from writing assignments that contained violent imagery, as was the case with the Virginia Tech killer and other shooters.

- Contrary to the popular belief that shooters are loners, only one-third were loners or thought to be; 41 percent socialized with mainstream students; only 12 percent had no close friends. A quarter of the shooters socialized with students disliked by mainstream kids or considered part of a fringe group. Forty-four percent were active in school activities in or outside of school.
- Nearly two-thirds of the shooters had never been in trouble while 27 percent had been suspended from school in the past.
- Most attackers (78 percent) showed some history of suicide

attempts, a history of thinking about it, or a history of depression.

- More than 50 percent had been documented in the past as feeling exceptionally depressed.
- Only 34 percent had ever received a mental health evaluation. Of those, 17 percent had been diagnosed with mental health or behavioral disorders prior to their attack.
- Nearly all of the attackers had experienced some type of loss prior to their event. Around 66 percent felt they had lost status in some way.
- Half had lost a loved one or lost an important relationship. About 15 percent had experienced an illness or someone close to them had been ill.
- Nearly all of the attackers (95 percent) planned their shootings—some just one or two days prior, while others thought about it for a year.
- Some 71 percent of the shooters felt bullied, persecuted, threatened, attacked, or injured prior to their school attack. In a few cases, these incidents had occurred over a long period of time; some had been severe.
- The one common denominator? In every case examined for the report, the attacker was male.

Indicators Often Ignored

Contrary to what people often claim, school shooters don't just suddenly change from being nonviolent to violent. The path is a progressive one with indicators along the way, ones that friends, fellow students, teachers, and parents often ignore. The Secret Service study showed that 93 percent of the attackers acted in such a way *prior* to the event that it concerned people. In one blatant example, an attacker asked his friends to help him get ammunition. Another told his friends several times that he thought about killing students at the school.

The percentages noted above are frightening because there are no flashing red lights or highlighted indicators. Many, many students fall within these percentages but don't carry out mass shootings. However, we cannot ignore some percentages. For example, 71 percent of the shooters were bullied, a serious issue that schools are making an effort to address. Some better than others.

Consider two boys in Green Bay, Wisconsin, one 17 years old, the other 18. Both weighed 300 pounds each, both complained of bullying and harassment, and both, according to one of the mothers, had been "pushed to the limit. They couldn't handle it anymore." One had been kicked out of the school the year before for carrying a knife for protection. His mother said she had called the principal and even a counselor to ask for help, but no one called her back.

Police arrested the boys after being tipped that they planned to

One Who Did Fit the Stereotype

It's been said that in every myth there is a degree of truth. On Oct. 10, 2007, 14-year-old Asa Coon walked into Success Tech Academy, in Cleveland, Ohio, and shot two teachers and two students before shooting himself to death. According to police and school records, as well as statements from neighbors, Coon had many problems:

- He was constantly teased. He had an unfortunate name as a white student in a predominately black school and was described as "kind of a chubby" goth who wore black trench coats, black fingernail polish, chains, and a dog collar.
- He was described as a poor student, a loner, and an angry kid.
- He had been diagnosed as possibly bipolar, but he refused to take his medication.
- Prior to the shooting, he had made threats to shoot those who teased him; few took those threats seriously, including the principal.

set off bombs near the bathrooms, set the exits on fire with jellied gasoline, and then shoot people who they didn't like. The police found nine rifles and shotguns, a pistol, 20 explosive devices, camouflage clothing, gas masks, two-way radios and hundreds of rounds of ammunition at the home of one of the boys. One of them said they had planned the killing for years.

There is also the issue of staff not taking action because they believe that the kid will somehow change or that nothing will come of it. One teacher told me that she had an obvious sociopath in her classroom, but since the boy had yet to do anything monumental—though everyone believed it was just a matter of time before he did—the school could not take action. The boy is still attending and acting out in mainstream classrooms.

ENDNOTE

1. "A year after Minn. shootings, questions, pain remain fresh." By Judy Keen. USA Today online. www.usatoday.com. Posted March 20, 2006. Accessed April 11, 2008.

Chapter 2

Prevention

The violence that walked in through the door that day really came out of nowhere.
> —Donna Varrica, spokesperson for Dawson College in Montreal, Canada, where on Sept. 13, 2006, a student shot 21 people, killing one.

I've heard some version of the above quote a thousand times during my police career. "The guy came out of nowhere and was suddenly hitting me." "This guy came out of nowhere and demanded my car keys." Oh really? Someone actually came out of nowhere? I don't mean to belittle these victims' perceptions, but the fact is that it's almost impossible for someone to come out of nowhere. In most cases they were there; the victim just didn't notice. (However, the case of the February 2008 shootings at Northern Illinois University was an exception in which the shooter did almost appear from "nowhere." He stepped out from behind a curtain in a lecture hall and began shooting students in the front row, who had no time to react.)

I specialized in white supremacy crimes and skinhead street gangs when I worked in the Portland (Oregon) Police Bureau's Gang Enforcement Team. On one occasion, I went to a high school to talk to the principal about information I had received that he had at least one racist skinhead attending who was committing racially motivated crimes.

The principal admonished me as if I were a freshman, clearly offended that I would even think that he might not have total control over what was happening on his turf. "I pride myself in knowing my flock," he said rather pompously. "I have eyes and ears in every corridor; I'm always in the know. There are no skinheads in my school. I would *never* allow it."

I apologized for taking his time and turned to make my exit. When I pushed open the door, which opened out into a crowded hallway, it bumped it into a passersby's shoulder, a kid with a shaved head, wearing a flight jacket covered with swastikas, camouflage pants, and Doc Martens boots. In other words, a skinhead.

No matter if you're a teacher, parent, or student, always keep this thought in mind: just because you don't *think* there isn't a problem doesn't mean there isn't one.

THE INDICATORS ARE THERE

Kids have been gossiping about another kid named Dan. They use words like "weird," "spaz," and "freaky." He used to be normal, they say, buy lately he's been keeping to himself. He has an Internet blog on which he talks incessantly about terrorists, especially about suicide bombers. It's like he admires them, they say. Most of the kids ignore him, although some tease him and call him names. Even the teachers talk about him in their break room. But not one kid, not one teacher, or not one counselor has talked to Dan to see what is going on in his life.

Should he one day wreak havoc on his school, how many people will say, "He just came out of nowhere"?

A Case Study

Had anyone been watching Cho Seung-Hui, the 23-year-old Virginia Tech student who killed 33 people and wounded another 25? They should have; the English major was practically carrying a neon sign that warned of the horrific event that was to come.

Cho had displayed indicators of violence for quite a while. He had set fire to a dorm room and had reportedly stalked women. A piece of writing found in his dorm, and believed to be written by him, reviled what he called "deceitful charlatans," "debauchery," and "rich kids."

At least one teacher had found Cho's work so disturbing that he was referred to the counseling center at the school. Did Cho go? No one knows because no one followed up.

It's believed that he was taking anti-depressant medication sometime in the past. Did he go off of it? No one knows for sure.

Had anyone been watching Cho?

How many said after the slaughter that "he just came out of nowhere"?

During the 1990s, there were 323 school-associated violent death shootings in the United States, resulting in 358 fatalities. Based on those incidents in which there was data, most of the firearms used in these killings were taken from the shooters' homes or from the homes of relatives or friends.

While teachers and staff have a good idea of what is happening on the campus, it's the kids who have the closest contact with others and, therefore, it's the kids who are in the best position to see and hear all that is going on. Sometimes, though, their lack of maturity to decipher or understand what they perceive, or their concern about being thought of as a snitch, means that important information is not given to an adult. Let's look at some ways to help the kids do the right thing.

Teach Kids to Trust Their Gut Feelings

Beginning when they are old enough to understand, kids are warned about predators. We tell them that they should never be pressured to give adults affection and we teach them about good touching and bad touching. Kids are told that when they feel funny or weird about an adult, they should tell another whom they trust.

But while we prepare our kids for a school year by buying them a new pair of shoes and a binder, we fail to say anything about other kids who might want to hurt them. Bullies. Kids with mental problems. Kids who say they have weapons in their backpacks. Kids who say they want to hurt others. Kids who, in a frightening way, don't act like the others.

For our purposes, a gut feeling is that intuitive inner voice that communicates good or bad data to us. These feelings come from our inner self where there occurs a rapid processing of incoming verbal data and body language information that we know from past experience is meaningful as far as predicting the behavior of people toward us and others. Sometimes it's accurate and sometimes it isn't.

Do Young Kids Have Gut Feelings?

Logic would tell us that very young kids, five or six years old, don't have gut feelings because they have yet to accumulate sufficient life experiences. While this might be generally true, there are still those little ones who are savvier than the norm, savvier than what we give them credit for.

One expert counselor, who is also a veteran teacher, retired school principal, and educational consultant, told me that she has found that even some kindergarten kids have gut feelings. As an example, she said that on one occasion she was supervising kindergartners on the playground when a child pointed out a man at the outer corner of the field who had been watching them.

"As Principal, I alerted my staff to begin watching for him in order to determine a pattern. And sure enough, he ended up being a child predator. I would never question a child's perceptions until I checked it out. Certainly, kids do not have as much experience as we do, but I believe that they do have an innate sense of danger, just as those in the animal kingdom. Investigating a child's claim is of utmost importance in that they often do color their world with a vivid imagination, but much of what kids talk about has some element of truth. Of course, most children older than this have even more refined instincts.

"Middle school children and certainly high school students usually know what is going on before us older folks do in that they often have such a great amount of street sense. Just watch them at your local mall or in any other public place. They are very alert and aware of their environment. Interviews with kids of all ages who have been in school shootings have validated this fact."

One teacher told me that we must teach young children how to listen to those instincts. "Adults feel gut instincts and kids feel gut instincts," she said, "but adults know what to do with them; kid's don't. Kids may feel it, but that doesn't mean they know what to do with it. Very young children can be told that there is a weird tingly sensation deep in their stomach that's different than a stomachache. When they feel that, they need to get away and tell someone."

Whether you call it a gut feeling, ESP, or a sixth sense, it's important to believe in it and to believe that kids can have it at any age no matter what their accumulated life experience. Author Litany Burns writes in *The Sixth Sense of Children: Nurturing Your Child's Intuitive Abilities* (NAL Trade, February 1, 2002), "From the moment they first enter the physical world as infants, they spontaneously rely on their sixth sense for communication and protection. It is what they innately know. Like animals, they rely on these primary unspoken impressions for their physical daily survival before language, mental and social skills have developed.

We aren't talking about an eerie supernatural ability in the sense of spooky movies, but rather a natural part of their being. Burns says: "There are millions of very normal intuitive children playing, working, sleeping and dreaming all over the world today. They play in city streets, on the fields of farmlands or in suburban backyards. They are poor and rich; black, white, yellow and brown; short and tall; male and female. Physical background does not limit their special abilities. Each child's sixth sense is as natural as loving, learning and breathing. The point here is that we must not write off young children's feelings about someone, such as that schoolyard predator mentioned earlier, or one child's feelings about another student acting or saying things perceived "funny" or "scary."

When do you act on a child's feelings? There is no answer to that. You have to trust *your* gut feelings.

Children need to learn that their instincts are important. It's important for us as parents and teachers that we don't teach kids to devalue their instincts simply because they cannot touch, see, or hear them. In light of all that is going on today in our schools, it's more important than ever for kids to use every advantage they have. We must not squash their powerful natural intuitive abilities.

LAYING THE GROUNDWORK WITH YOUR CHILD

The days have long passed of assuming that our schools are safe places for our children. Today, perhaps more than ever before, there is a possibility that a menace might pass through the doors in the form of an angry parent, a mentally ill adult, or a student seeking to target his or her rage and despair on innocent classmates.

To refuse to take preventive measures, to fail to see the need to think strategically, and to refuse to prepare for any possibility is simply wrong and irresponsible. Yes, there are 119,000 public and private schools and the odds are high that it won't happen at yours.

But it might. The odds were high that it would never happen at a sleepy university in Virginia. But it did. The odds were even higher that it would never ever happen in an Amish school in Pennsylvania. But it did.

The statistics and the daily news make it clear: The time for denial is over. If you're a student, being prepared is a must. If you're a teacher or a parent, being prepared should be in your job description.

Before Sending Your Kids to School

Before sending your kids off to school, give them some guidelines about sensible behavior and awareness:

- Show respect for fellow students, teachers, principals, and other school staff.
- Avoid teasing and name-calling. It might seem fun, but it probably isn't to the target of the insult. Some will be hurt and angered by it.
- Steer clear of fights. It might be exciting to watch a fight in the hall or outside the school, but someone might have a weapon. A bullet stops when it hits something or someone. Don't stop to watch; walk away quickly and inform an adult.
- Listen for teachers' instructions in an emergency.
- Be careful who you hang out with. Being a member of a gang can get you hurt, even killed, it can give you a bad reputation, and it may limit your friends to only gang members.
- Try to talk out problems instead of fighting.
- Know where you would run if there was sudden violence in the cafeteria, hallway, playground, library, and gym.
- Speak up. Tell a parent, bus driver, cafeteria cook, teacher, coach, or security officer if another student is harassing you.
- Tell an adult immediately if you know someone has a weapon.

Making Confident Kids

Your kids aren't likely to talk to you about what is going on at school if you haven't laid the groundwork so that they *want* to come to you. If you have always been too busy for them, if you have never talked with them face-to-face, and if you have never shown them that you're listening to what they say, how do you expect them to come to you, let alone even think of you should there be a serious issue at school?

Kids who are confident in themselves and confident that you're the person to talk to are more likely to do exactly that when they are worried or frightened about something. Here are some ways that you, as parents, can lay that foundation.

High School Kids

Mid to older teens want respect to enhance their sense of confidence. They see themselves as young adults and they want others, especially you, to see them that way. You might not like their purple hair, alien-like clothing, and their choice of friends, but if you respect them and they see that respect, you will instill in them a sense of confidence.

Middle School Kids

Kids 11 to 14 or 15 want your trust. Give it by allowing them to make choices and decisions on their own. You might not always like what they decide—changing their hair color, quitting the band, going out for basketball—but if they aren't likely to get hurt, just bite your tongue and let them make some decisions. Let them see that you trust them and then watch their confidence grow.

Grade School Kids

From kindergarten to about 11 years old, kids need complimentary words from you. They need praise and reassuring touches. They need to see your face and your eyes as you listen carefully to what they say, to whatever is on their minds. From that, they see that they are important, especially to you.

When you show older kids respect, allow young teens the chance to make their own decisions, and give youngsters your undivided attention, there is a greater chance that you will be the one they seek out to tell what is going on in their lives and at their school. This advice goes for teachers, too. When you treat your students this way, you're likely to be the one the kids trust to come to about suspicious activity or a potentially dangerous situation.

Teach Your Kids Responsibility

Blaming others for their problems is typical of kids (and parents) who have a propensity toward being confrontational, even to the extent of acting out violently. They are often vengeful, antagonistic, and feel that everyone is out to get them. They are convinced that teachers and the principal are quick to accuse them of things. Often their sense of paranoia is valid because their behavior makes it so. That is, their actions and demeanor create a self-fulfilling prophecy because the more argumentative and suspicious they become, the more other people accuse them of wrongdoing.

Bulletproof Backpacks

Two concerned fathers in Boston have put their inventive minds together to develop a bulletproof backpack for kids. Inspired and frightened by the Columbine school shooting in 1999, the inventors got an idea to place bulletproof material inside backpacks, which virtually every kid carries from kindergarten all the way through college; kids can use the straps as handles and hold the bag in front of themselves.

The company also offers lightweight bulletproof panels that can be inserted into any pack and 8 1/2 x 11 inch panels that fit into a three-ring binder for situations where a pack is not practical to carry. Visit www.mychildspack.com to see the whole line of products.

These kids are likely to use "they" and "everyone" in their speech. "They say I pushed Amy Brown down the stairs." "Everyone always thinks that I steal things." "They say I beat up Sammy at lunch time."

When I would ask a kid if, say, he did beat up Sammy, I would occasionally get a blank look and then a hesitant nod. I'd say, "Well, it looks like the 'they' people were right then." Even after a kid admitted that he was the culprit, the real issue to him was that others were blaming him for it. In his mind, that was more significant than the fact that he indeed committed the assault.

It's beyond the scope of this book to discuss ways to teach kids responsibility; indeed, it's the subject of many books, articles, and parenting classes. If as a parent you need help in teaching your kids how to take responsibility for their actions, please seek it out. It will make the difficult job of raising kids just a little easier.

To state the obvious to anyone raising children: Parenting is a tough job. I was blessed with three wonderful kids who are grown now and making their marks in the world. Still, raising them was hard.

Michael Carneal, a small and immature 14-year-old boy living in Paducah, Kentucky, who was later described by his lawyer as suffering from paranoia and a schizophrenia-like disorder, wrote stories and school essays about feeling weak and picked on his entire life. Did his parents ever see his writing or search his room? Did his teachers have concerns about his essays? Did he seem to come out of nowhere when he came to school with five guns and shot and killed three girls and wounded five others?

Worrying is what a parent does, hence the deep lines around the eyes. Worrying about your child getting shot at school never even used to be in a parent's radar. Not so today. Parenting a potential shooter didn't used to be a consideration, not even a remote one. But every shooter in the dozens of incidents mentioned in this book had parents.

Here are some things to think about:

- Naturally your defenses come up when you hear something negative about your child from the principal or a daycare worker. While such feelings are natural, strive to listen and to accept that there just might be a problem.
- All your hopes and dreams for your child will be for naught if you can't get beyond yourself. It's hard not to take it personally when your child is having problems; you think it reflects on your parenting. Well, it might indeed be your lack of parenting skills, but it can also be a separate issue. For the sake of your child, it's imperative that you investigate all possible causes.
- Talk to your child. Yes, it can be like pulling teeth from a chicken, but isn't it worth it? When he does talk, let him do so while you just listen.
- Consider the accusation. That your child got into trouble for cracking jokes in class is one thing, but it's something entirely different when he gets into trouble for packing a hammer in his backpack to thump someone.
- If your child is having problems mainly at home, consider taking him to a mental health practitioner. Get a referral from your pediatrician, find one online, in the Yellow Pages, or ask a friend. There is no shame in this. Wouldn't you take him to the doctor if he sprained his knee?
- If your child's problems are occurring in school, ask the school counselors for help. They might arrange a meeting for you, your child, his teachers, and other involved people. Once again, an open mind on your part is an absolute here. Being defensive, angry, and firing back counter accusations won't help.
- You also need to be open minded enough to determine if your child is potentially dangerous to you. If so, remove weapons from your house. Search his room, read his e-mail, and look

into his backpack. If you're afraid of him, do it when he isn't around. Those parents killed by school shooters should have. As a police officer, there were many occasions when I went to kids' bedrooms and found dangerous or incriminating things that the parents didn't know were there.

A Thought for Parents

One behavioral expert said that a child's beliefs, behaviors, and motivations should be completely transparent to the parent. If at any point they aren't—that is, the kid's behavior, motives and actions have become unclear—the parents need to do all they can to make them transparent again. Of course, there is going to be some of this in the teen years, so the parent should know the difference. When unsure, seek help.

ESTABLISHING A THREAT ASSESSMENT COMMITTEE

School threat assessment committees are superior programs compared to those of "zero tolerance" or student profiling, which often stigmatize innocent kids who have two or three characteristics on some behavioral checklist. Unfortunately, there isn't an established standard threat assessment model, but that isn't a problem because it isn't that difficult to develop.

Parents should call their child's school and see if it has a threat assessment program in effect; if your child's school doesn't have one, volunteer to lay the groundwork. Teachers and students should also work toward getting a threat assessment program started in their school.

What It Is

A threat assessment team consists of school personnel, to include administrators, mental health workers, and security staff. Local police officers should be included, as well as representatives of pertinent social service agencies. Their function is to investigate reported instances of threatening behavior and then make a determination as to the seriousness of the actions.

Besides providing a specific place where students, teachers, and even parents can report their concerns, the threat assessment team also works with potential offenders to alleviate their sense of hopelessness, depression, and rage. The team will have at its disposal access to resources to refer students, such as mental health programs and various social services. This is all done confidentially.

Is Local Law Enforcement Familiar with Your School?

Check with the administration to see if the neighborhood police officer has conducted a walk-through of your school. Although he might have been to the office a few times to deal with problems, invite the officer to familiarize himself with all the hall connections, locations of classrooms, library, cafeteria, parking lot, and various nooks and crannies.

Follow these steps to make it happen:

- Talk with the school principal about the idea.
- If the principal agrees, call the police precinct that serves the school and ask to talk with the commander.
- Or, when there is an on-campus police officer present at the school, talk with that person about getting the neighborhood patrol officer to conduct a walk-through. Although it's good that the school officer is familiar with the building, the regular district officer should be, too.
- If the principal refuses, present your proposal to the parent/teachers association. If they balk, contact the school district office. If they refuse, write your local newspaper and contact the local television media. Don't take no for an answer; your children's lives are at stake.

Many students who make threats never carry them out. Some students who seem the most threatening never make a threat.

With a threat assessment program in place, kids have a place, more specifically, a trusted adult, they can turn to. However, before they can do so, they need to know that the program exists. Inform students via school newsletter, homeroom presentations, and posters of the following details:

* The team exists, and it's user-friendly.
* Students are doing the right thing by reporting their concerns.
* The team consists of dedicated people who listen and take students' concerns seriously.
* Their concerns and information will be handled discreetly.
* Their information protects both the victim(s) and the potential shooter.

Criticism by Students

Will some students mock the idea of a threat assessment committee? Of course. That's what some kids do.

As a police officer, I heard every imaginable taunt come from the mouths of students whenever I stepped onto a campus, as have most other police officers. However, think about the news footage of school shootings you have seen over the past few years, and you might recall students clinging desperately to police officers as they were led to safety out of the schools. Even when out of the danger zone, many of these frightened students, including burly football players, had to be pried away from rescuing officers.

There might well be criticism of the committee, but people will use it when it's professional and it functions the way it promises.

Let students know that the members of the threat assessment team are trained to help them, and that they will use all their resources to accomplish the following goals:

- Treat every contact with respect, discretion, and seriousness.
- Document the threats.
- Evaluate the motivation of the complainant.
- Determine the intervention needed.
- Interview the alleged offender.
- Present the complaint to all members of the team.
- Bring in more experts as necessary, including mental health professionals and police.
- Take appropriate disciplinary action and/or law enforcement action.
- Implement security measures against the threat.
- Respond to media queries.
- Conduct a follow-up investigation.

This is a short overview of a threat assessment committee. The committee can be a simple group of three or four people or one that involves a dozen or more from a variety of community programs. No matter if the committee is large or small, it's important that everyone work in a collaborative effort, everyone learns from each other, and all work toward the same objective: prevention, facilitation, and help.

The Secret Service offers training on creating a safe school environment, preventing targeted violence, and responding to threatening situations. Go to www.secretservice.gov for the phone number of an office near you and ask them for information about preventing school violence.

<table>
<tr><td>**Chapter**

3</td><td># When a Student
Seems Dangerous</td></tr>
</table>

I said, "I don't want a Columbine or anything happening around here" . . . and now it has because I didn't say anything.
> —A parent who overheard his son's friend
> making threats during a Saturday night sleepover.
> The friend, Charles Andrew Williams, 15,
> told the man he was joking. Williams went into
> Santana High School in Santee, California, the following
> Monday and killed two classmates and wounded 13 others.[1]

Parents, what should your children do if they hear about or see someone talking or acting in a threatening manner? Should they look the other way? Ignore them? Offer friendship? Parentstalk.com asked school-age children what they would do in that situation following a school shooting in March 2001.[2] Here are some of their responses:

"If one of my friends brought a gun to school I would tell them not to do anything stupid."–Steven, Age 11

"I probably wouldn't take my friend seriously."–Britytany, Age 12

"I think that when a kid brings a gun to school it's just out of loneliness [or they] don't get enough attention at home . . ." –Christeena, Age 14

If this were a school assignment, these kids would all get an F.

IF YOUR CHILD KNOWS SOMEONE HAS A GUN

While kids tell us that they take guns, knives, and assorted bludgeons to school for self-protection, to threaten someone, or to feel superior (reasons that might sound rational to them), you must make it clear to your children that kids should never bring a weapon onto the campus. In fact, kids should never be in possession of a gun or knife anywhere—period. Drill this into their heads.

I emphasize this because during my years working gang enforcement, there were countless kids who told me that they thought it was OK to have a gun or knife handy in a backpack, pocket, or locker when someone deemed it necessary for protection. I even had cases where parents gave their kids weapons to carry for self-defense. Wrong. Never. Ever. At no time.

Elsewhere in this book, we examine ways to recognize and use various objects found in a classroom and throughout the campus for self-defense. These are common objects found in the school environment—staplers, chairs, backpacks—that are legal and far less likely to hurt innocent people.

Now that you have ingrained this into your kids' gray matter, you must do some additional embedding as to what they must do should they see or hear about a weapon in another student's possession. Here are the easy steps:

Where Do Kids Get Guns?

According to the U.S. Secret Service National Threat Assessment Center, two thirds of the school shooters got their guns from their home or a relative's home. There were even some cases where kids were given guns as gifts from their parents.

Even when they couldn't find guns at home, they were able to find them elsewhere. The Coalition to Stop Gun Violence estimates there are 192 million guns in private hands in this country.

- **If they see someone with a weapon, they need to get away from that person quickly.** If they know of someone who might have a weapon, they must avoid him. Young children and even some teens don't understand that a missed shot will *always* hit something—or someone. There was an incident in my city where a gunman shot at someone on 6th Avenue but the missed round traveled all the way to 3rd Avenue, where it struck and killed a man walking with his wife.
- **If they know that someone has a weapon, they should tell a teacher, a staff person, or security.** Not tomorrow or next Tuesday—tell them today. If for whatever reason your child is adamant about not telling an adult face-to-face, tell him to make an anonymous phone call to the office or to someone on the Threat Assessment Committee (see Chapter 2). Or call 9-1-1. If your child wants, he can ask that his name be kept confidential. Is telling tough for some kids to do? Yes. So find the best way you know to impress upon your kids the importance of letting someone know. In many school shootings, investigators found students who reported that they knew the shooter had access to guns long before the incident.

In the Tech Success Academy shooting, a student walked into a school restroom where the shooter was loading his weapon. When he saw what the gunman was doing, he exited the room but didn't tell anyone. "I don't know what I was thinking," he said later after the shooter had gunned down four people before killing himself.

- **They must tell you.** Maybe they are afraid that you will "make a scene" and embarrass them, or make the situation dangerous. In the mind of a 12- or 15-year-old, this is a legitimate concern and you need to be open to discuss it with them.

But you need to make them understand that it's not up for a long discussion because every second there is a kid at school with a gun, there is risk.

What You Want Your Kids to Report

Talk to your kids about what you, the staff, and the police need to know:

- What did you see and where did you see it? Example: You saw a boy named Jace displaying a handgun in his waistband to several other students outside the front cafeteria doors at noon. Or you heard Amy say she had her father's gun in her locker. Or you heard a rumor that Danny was learning how to make explosives from the Internet.
- Did you hear a rumor? Adults must decide if it is just a joke or a lie. A child should never try to make such a determination.
- What do you know about the kid with a gun? What is his full name, his homeroom, age, height, weight, the clothing he wore on the day you saw him with the weapon, what car does he drive, and who does he hang out with?
- If you want to be anonymous, demand it.

When a Student Threatens from Home

Your child calls you from school and says she heard that a student, John, who has been absent all week, has been making threats from his home to take a gun to school and "do a Virginia Tech on everyone." She has been hearing this for a week and just this afternoon she learned from a friend that John has been text-messaging people all day about having two guns.

What Do You Do as a Parent?

Call the police. Tell them the nature of the threat, what your daughter knows about John, and the exact words he used. Let them know if he has talked previously about owning guns.

Next, call the school so they can decide what needs to be done on the campus, such as closing the school, implementing a lockdown, asking the police to come onto the site, coordinating efforts with school security, and calling parents. Do not assume that your earlier call to the police will result in them immediately calling the school.

Let's say you're a parent at home and John calls your daughter who is with you and informs her of his plan. She scribbles notes as he speaks, and you learn that John is telling her that he has weapons and plans to go to school to shoot students and teachers. Use your cell to call 9-1-1 as your child continues to keep him talking and getting information. Read to the police everything she writes down: his address, his location in the house, any indication of being high on drugs, threats to kill himself, and the type(s) of weapon(s) he says he has. If he hangs up, let the police know so they can consider sending officers to the school.

What Do You Do as a Student?

Immediately inform an adult, a teacher, someone in the office, or call the police. Tell them everything you know about the situation. If you're concerned about your safety, ask them to keep your identity anonymous.

Let's say you're a student somewhere by yourself and John calls to tell you of his plan. Keep him on the phone as you note as much information as you can get out of him. Then when you hang up, immediately call the police.

Depending on the laws in your jurisdiction, the police might or might not arrest the caller. If they can't for legal reasons, at least they are involved, which will hopefully intimidate the caller into stopping his threatening behavior. It also establishes a record of the incident with the police in the event there are future threats.

Is It a Joke or a Stupid Rumor?

When is a kid just making empty threats out of anger? When is a comment to be taken as a joke?

Parents, tell your kids that because school shootings and mass killings on campus have become all too regular, we must take such talk seriously—always. Kids must understand that any concerns over getting someone in trouble or over-reacting need to be set aside. Would they rather feel uncomfortable for telling and then everything turned out to be OK, or feel devastated for not telling and then several classmates lose their lives?

Let them know that it's not up to them to decide how legitimate a threat is. Their responsibility is to tell an adult and let them handle it.

Telling Is OK

Talk with your kids ahead of time about the importance of telling you about potentially dangerous situations and the threats of dangerous situations. Discuss with them that telling in this case will keep people from getting hurt.

The issue of telling isn't as negative among grade school kids as it is with those in middle school and high school. The task, and it can definitely be a task, is to convince teens that it's OK to tell.

Straight Talk to Teens

You're just a few years from being an adult and it's time to drop the teens-versus-adults thinking. Your parents, teachers, principal, and security staff are not your enemy. They are interested in seeing you succeed and being the best young person and, eventually, the best adult you can be. They are there to point the way and help you over the rough spots. Sure, you want to be independent and responsible for your path, but don't let that create a mentality that prevents you from doing the right thing. Tell an adult when you see or hear something about a weapon, explosives, a hit list, arson, or anything else that might hurt you and your friends. Sure, you can take care of yourself, so do it for those teens who aren't quite there yet.

Do your best and hope that while it might appear that they are dismissing your advice, they really are hearing you.

It's paramount that kids understand that they must immediately get away from the armed kid and go straight to an adult. Here are some ideas to impress upon your child:

- Tell your child to never assume that the kid is just showing off or that it's OK because he needs a weapon for protection. Consider that the kid might be actively looking to threaten or hurt someone, or several people. Ingrain in your child all the way to her marrow that no kid should ever bring a weapon to school.
- If your child sees the weapon, she should get completely out of the area.
- Your child should immediately tell an adult, teacher, principle, counselor, or visiting parent. She should tell them what she saw, who she saw, where it happened, what type of weapon the person displayed, what they said, and what they were doing. Tell her to call you if she can't find anyone else to report the incident to.
- If your child has to talk to the police, she can ask them to keep her name confidential.
- Your child should write down what she saw in detail—name of the person in question, what he said, what he did, what he had in his possession, or what he said he had—and who she reported it to. This helps her remember the details should she need to talk about them later.

HOW TO TALK TO AN UPSET OR VOLATILE PERSON

Should an emotionally upset student become enraged and begin making overt threats at one or more people—"You'll be sorry. I'm going to get my father's gun and come back here and blow you away!"—or, conversely, he becomes suddenly quiet and makes veiled threats—"I got something for y'all"—a teacher, counselor, or even another student might want to approach him. Whether this is a good idea depends on the situation, the intensity of the threat, the emotional state of the person wanting to intervene, and many other factors discussed throughout this book.

If the student's anger is directed at a specific teacher, that teacher should not approach the student. If another student wants to step up to talk with the upset person, it's important that he is mature, a competent talker, and has a real interest in calming the agitated person and encouraging him to seek help. Most often, this will be a student of high school or college age, although there might be exceptions in lower grades.

Maintain a Cool Demeanor

Don't show anger, nervousness, or fear as it just might agitate the student more. Draw on your acting experience to stand calmly, hands up, palms toward the student, your face expressionless. Talk in a lower tone than the upset student's, keeping your voice even and without emotion. Maintain this demeanor no matter what he says. Don't use a condescending tone and don't challenge his

Weapon's Cache with Mom's Support

The day after Asa Coon shot up his school in Cleveland, Ohio, another 14-year-old boy was arrested in Plymouth Township near Philadelphia for suspicion of planning a Columbine-type shooting at a Pennsylvania high school. Police officers found dozens of weapons in the boy's bedroom, including an operational hand grenade, three additional hand grenades under construction, and various manuals.

Police arrested the boy's mother after learning that she had bought three of the weapons at a gun show. The investigation revealed that the parents had been indulging the boy because he was unhappy. Authorities didn't believe they knew of his plans.

motives. If you feel you aren't helping or that you're making matters worse, back off.

Don't Tell Him to "Calm Down"

This request never calms anyone. In fact, it's likely to anger the student further since it's often perceived as passing judgment.

Ask How You Can Help

Place the burden of the moment on yourself. "How can I help?" This carries much more power than "What's the matter with *you*?" Expect that he just might dump all his problems on you; he might even start yelling. This is fine if it helps him vent.

Listen to Him

Watch how TV news reporters interview people. They nod, they look the person in the eyes, and they stay neutral no matter what the person says. That is what you want to do. Nodding doesn't mean you agree with what he is saying; it just means you're hearing him. That might be all he wants.

Listen to His Complaint

Something has driven the student to this extreme. He might even have a good solution to his issue. At the very least, his venting might calm his agitated mind.

Watch What You Say

Don't say anything to embarrass him or to push his volatile emotions further. You can't go wrong by simply nodding and saying, "Yes," "I see," and "I understand." Your role is to diffuse his emotions, not necessarily solve his issue.

When you're finished, follow through with any promises you made. Talk to a teacher, counselor, or principal about the student's problems. Think about what you can do to alleviate any legitimate concerns he has about being the victim of continuous ridicule, bullying, harassment, and so on. If it's an issue that is widespread, talk to counselors and teachers about forming a committee that works to quell these problems on campus. Know that you can't fix everything, but work to do what you can.

SHOULD WE PAY STUDENTS FOR INFORMATION?

Some school administrators have experimented with paying students for information about other students making threats, and bringing drugs, alcohol, or weapons onto school grounds. Those in favor of it say that some kids won't come forward just because it's the right thing to do but will if there is a $50 payoff. They argue that in most of the well-publicized shootings, the gunman gave hints or said overtly what he was planning to do. Therefore, a money reward might encourage students to let someone know and possibly avert another tragedy.

Students at one school felt that the program insulted their integrity by assuming that they needed payment to do the right thing. Others thought it would lead to abuse by unscrupulous students filing false reports for the money. Still others hope we can evolve to where we don't have to pay people. There are no figures as to the success or failure of paying students for information.

THE PROBLEM WITH ZERO TOLERANCE

In light of increasing incidents of school violence as well as school shootings, school district governing boards have adopted what is termed "zero tolerance" policies toward violent behavior, violent incidents, and any crime in general. Not tolerated would be infractions such as robbery, extortion, possession of drugs or weapons, assault, or causing serious injury to another. Violation of these rules could lead to expulsion when other means to fix the problem had failed or the situation is such that there is risk to others.

While at first blush the concept would appear to be a good

thing, its implementation has received mixed reviews. Opponents say that it enacts punishment, some say harsh punishment, for any violation of school rules without exceptions and without any consideration of mitigating circumstances. Here are some examples:

- A third-grade boy was suspended after he drew a picture of a soldier holding a canteen and a knife and brought this picture to school.
- A 12-year-old boy who said he brought powdered sugar to school for a science project was charged with a felony for possessing a look-alike drug.
- A security guard chased a suspected burglar armed with a knife into an elementary school. However, school officials deemed the security guard the criminal since he carried an otherwise legal pistol onto school property, and had him arrested for felony possession of a weapon on school property.
- Some schools have banned kids from playing "cops and robbers," threatening them with expulsion out of fear that even imaginary weapons pose a threat.
- An 11-year-old was suspended after she folded a piece of paper into the shape of a gun.
- A 6-year-old was suspended for taking home a plastic knife from the school cafeteria. He wasn't threatening; he just wanted to show his mother he had learned how to spread butter on his bread.
- A prosecutor in one jurisdiction met with school officials to insist that all threats, no matter how minor, be cause for automatic suspensions and referrals to the district attorney.

One teacher said that while many schools have a no-tolerance policy, the problem isn't with the guidelines but with those who enforce them. She says that when a student configures a gun with his hand and points it at someone, she doesn't call their parents or kick them out of the class. She simply asks them not to do it and that ends that.

Parents, attorneys, and assorted groups and organizations are taking a hard look at zero tolerance programs and working to find a more fair way, a less hysterical way, to address problems in our schools. But that won't give any comfort to the children who have been the victims of arbitrary policies that have administered extreme punishment in the name of school safety. As one National Merit scholar said after she was jailed and banned from her graduation for leaving a kitchen knife in her car that she had been using to open boxes, "They're taking away my memories."

SHOULD WE ARM TEACHERS?

You're a high school senior sitting in history class when you hear a cluster of shots from outside the door. Although you're not aware of it right now, you will remember later that you saw the teacher off to your left drop down behind his desk. Then there is another cluster of shots just before a figure, someone dressed in camouflage pants and a black jacket, steps through the open door to your right and points a handgun at the classroom.

A loud bang from your left confuses you. Then another.

To your right, the figure in cammo drops his gun and slumps against the door. He remains there for a moment before he crumples to the floor, motionless.

Your teacher, the nerdy Mr. Gleason, had been carrying a gun. He had trained with it and been certified to carry it legally.

And he just saved the lives of everyone in the classroom.

The opinions are many as to whether teachers should carry firearms. Would Columbine have ended earlier with fewer lives lost if a staff member had shot one or both killers? How about at Virginia Tech University? How about at dozens of other school shootings?

Some people are alarmed at the very thought of armed teachers on campus. They say, "What if a child gets the gun?" "What if an armed teacher shoots himself in the foot?" But others say,

"What if half a dozen students die in a classroom while an unarmed teacher stands by helplessly?" Of these three questions, the last one has already happened—repeatedly.

Gun-free school zones have made schools into one of the very few places, at least in this country, where would-be killers know that they won't face armed victims who can fight back and save lives.

In October 2007, conservative syndicated columnist Michelle Malkin wrote an online blog entry about Shirley Katz, a teacher in Oregon who had sought permission to bring her gun to school because she feared her ex-husband.[3] "Our safety plan at our school now is that if somebody threatening comes in, you try to avoid eye contact, and do whatever they say, and that is not acceptable anymore," said Katz. The following comments were left by readers of Malkin's blog; they have been lightly edited for clarity:

"It's kind of obvious about the risk of putting a weapon in a teacher's hand and God forbid you have a student who gets ahold of it."

"I can't understand why a responsible adult can't be armed in a school zone. . . . Just think what a properly trained and armed teacher could have done at Columbine. As long as an individual meets the CCW [carry concealed weapon] law (normally age 21) requirements to include the training required, why not let them carry in a college environment? Recent history shows there is no place more dangerous for a law abiding person than a gun-free zone."

"Security in my area consists of a potbellied [security guard] ambling down the halls."

> Why hasn't there been a mass shooting by a gunman at a police station? Might it be because people there carry guns and would shoot back?

"I'm a teacher; I'm not a gun owner. But it's foolish in this day and age to not allow someone who has gone through the process of obtaining a concealed carry license from carrying it into a school. If someone truly has evil intent, there isn't going to be anyone to stop them in the schools."

"A police officer assigned to every school is expensive and most likely won't prevent an attack. There were cops on campus at Virginia Tech but by the time they reached the scene, 33 people were dead."

"The whole notion of a bunch of private citizens walking around packing concealed heat in anticipation of a modern day shootout at the O.K. Corral just makes me kind of queasy."

I'll end this section by making two comments on the last quote. First, just because someone chooses to submit to a criminal records check, a background investigation, buy an expensive weapon and be trained to use and carry it, doesn't mean they anticipate a "shootout at the O.K. Corral." While there might be that rare individual who does, most carry for their personal safety, the safety of their family, and the safety of others.

When my city, Portland, Oregon, first allowed people to apply for a concealed gun permit (which meant a mandatory background search, a criminal history check, and mandatory training), I was apprehensive, as were most officers. I thought: "Now there will be even more guns on the street in the hands of nitwits."

But none of the things we dreaded came to pass. People

Israel's Solution

In the mid 1970s in Israel, many civilians were shot by terrorists armed with machine guns. However, when laws allowed Israeli citizens to carry concealed handguns, terrorists quickly discovered ordinary people pulling weapons on them in self-defense. In short order, terrorists in Israel no longer engaged in public shootings.

There was one shooting of school children in March of 1997 when a Jordanian soldier shot and killed seven Israeli girls as they visited Jordan's Island of Peace. There was no return fire, no self-defense, because the Israelis had complied with Jordanian requests to leave their weapons behind when they entered the border enclave.

Several parents of the girls said they might have been able to stop the shooting if they had had their weapons.

weren't drawing their weapons at every slight provocation, and there were no incidents of the wrong people getting the guns and using them. However, we did have several incidents of people using their weapons to stop a crime from occurring. This has been the case in many other jurisdictions.

Adrian Alan, a police officer in South Dakota, wrote this in a letter to the editor of the *Badger Herald*, in Madison, Wisconsin:

"Those who oppose this law will try to claim that there will be gunfights, people will look for fights and 'blood will run in the streets.' In my professional experience, and after significant research I've completed on concealed-carry laws in other states, this is simply not true. In fact, I have not been able to find a single state that has legalized concealed carry in the last 50 years and has turned around and re-criminalized it. In fact, I have found concealed-carry permit holders in most states are far less likely to be involved in criminal activity than other citizens."

There is much to discuss on this issue, especially if we could agree that some teachers be allowed to carry:

- Which teachers will be eligible?
- How much initial training should they get?
- How much ongoing training should they get?
- What kind of weapon should they carry?
- How would they carry it?
- In what situation would they use it?
- What would be the political ramifications?
- What would be the ramifications with those parents who opposed it?
- What would be the school's liability? The teacher's liability?

As I began writing this, several months had passed since 33 people died at Virginia Tech and the debate about arming teachers had begun to lose intensity. Then came the shootings at Northern Illinois University, and the debate began again.

ENDNOTES

1. "Student kills 2 classmates, wounds 13 near San Diego." CNN online. http://archives.cnn.com/2001/US/03/05/school.shooting.05/index.html. Posted March 5, 2001. Accessed July 10, 2008.
2. Parents-Talk.com. What Kids Think. "Guns in School." http://www.parents-talk.com/kidseyes/ke_wkt_shooting.html. Accessed April 17, 2008.
3. "Why should teachers be exempt from the Second Amendment?" By Michelle Malkin, www.michellemalkin.com. Posted October 8, 2007. Accessed April 14, 2008.

Chapter 4

Mind-Set and Strategy

All things are ready, if our minds be so.
—William Shakespeare, *Henry V*

Let's look at a mental tool that soldiers and police officers have used for years. By understanding and using this powerful way of thinking and seeing everything around you, you dramatically increase your ability to react without surprise to a violent incident in your school. Since you "see it coming," you're better able to follow the plan you have rehearsed in your mind.

STAGES OF ALERTNESS

Condition White
This is a state of environmental unawareness; that is, your head is buried in the sand. You don't know what's going on around you because you're daydreaming, tired, or distracted, or you believe that violence would never happen at your school. Condition White is OK at home, but it isn't OK anywhere else.

Condition Yellow
When you are in Condition Yellow, you're more alert. You're

relaxed, but you're alert and aware of everything that is going on all around you. (At first, this might be a little hard to do, but within a week you'll be doing it without even thinking about it.) You're so watchful that your total awareness makes you notice anything that might be suspicious or make you uncomfortable, no matter how minor. Yellow is the lowest level of awareness you should have when you're at school.

Condition Orange

Trouble rears its ugly head. Something causes you to utter, "Uh-oh." Someone calls out that a student has pulled a weapon of some kind out of his backpack near the office and is shouting that he is "going to get the office staff." Your decision as to what to do is based on the actual situation, how close you are to the action, any training you have received from your school, parents, police, and this book, how much danger you are in, your experience in handling a high-risk situation, and your gut feeling. You might decide to run away, help get others out of the area, lock the doors, call 9-1-1, or grab something to use as a weapon. Whatever action you take—based on prior thinking, planning, and mental rehearsal—will depend on the situation. If you find yourself starting to "lose it"—shake, hyperventilate, cry, scream—you need to begin four-count combat breathing (discussed later in this chapter) to slow your breathing and heart rate so you can think clearly.

It's much easier to move from Condition Yellow to Condition Orange or even jump to Condition Red than it is to move from the total unawareness of Condition White to Orange or Red.

Condition Red

It's happening! You must react now. Depending on what is happening and where, you're either going to run or you're going to have to fight. The student is about 20 feet from you as he stands clutching a handgun and looking at the office door. You have this kid in one of your classes but you have never seen him look like this: glassy eyes, sweating profusely, his face hard and his intention clear. Can you jump him? Are there people here who would help? Is there something available to hit him with when he looks the other way? Or should you shout at everyone to get away from him, which would likely draw his attention to you? Whatever he is doing and in whatever way you respond, it's all happening now.

Now is Condition Red. If you have planned for this moment, if you have thought about it, talked about, read about it, and practiced for it in live drills on the campus and in your mind using mental imagery, your decisions and actions are likely to be smooth, smart, and lifesaving.

Be Yellow

Is it paranoia to maintain Condition Yellow throughout your day? No. It's smart.

It involves a little conscious effort the first week or two, but after that Condition Yellow becomes a natural place to be. It's similar to when you first began driving. At first you were intentionally alert, aware, and conscious of all the details. However, after a while you no longer had to make a deliberate effort. Being alert, aware, and conscious of details is just something you do when you drive.

The same is true of Condition Yellow. After an initial intentional effort, you no longer have to work at it. You're naturally quick to notice things out of the norm and quick to pick up on subtle cues from people. Condition Yellow dramatically increases your reaction time and the likelihood of responding effectively.

Condition Black

Condition Black is one of panic, absolute terror, frozen muscles, frozen thinking—and getting hurt. This most often happens to those who walk around in Condition White, people who had no idea there was danger around until it was too late. To avoid this, you must always be in Condition Yellow at school. You must be aware of the possibility of violence there, plan for it, visualize your response to it in your mind, discuss it with trusted classmates, and always—always—be alert and aware of what is going on around you.

EXAMINE YOUR SCHOOL STRATEGICALLY

Your kids know where to go in the school office when they need to copy a document or get more paper clips. They know where to go in the gym to find the coach or to get a towel. But do they know where to go should someone casually stroll along the main hall, a gun in each hand, mouth slack, eyes dead, and firing into the face of anyone he confronts? Or where to go in the parking lot should a distraught, knife-wielding student begin slashing insanely?

Later in this chapter, we discuss visualizing violent situations in your children's school and ways for them to respond. But to visualize with detail, your children first need to analyze their surroundings as a battleground, a place where they might have to run, hide, even fight for their life. Thinking about it from that point of view, the school takes on a whole new look.

You must talk to your children about this method of preparation. If they are very young, consider making your discussion a silly game. "If a purple gorilla was chasing you in this hall, where would you go to get away? To hide? To get help?" In the turmoil of a school shooting, they might very well remember their answers. If your kids are in middle school or high school, your approach will be more sophisticated. At this age they might ignore or rebuff your questions and comments as to their preparation, but discuss it with them anyway with the hope that it will sink in.

Here are a few aspects of your children's school environment that you must consider in your conversation with them:

Examine the Exits

- How many are near where you are right now?
- Where are they?
- What is on the other side of each door?
- Can the doors be locked?
- Can they be fortified with chairs, cabinets, lockers?
- Do they have windows? Curtains?
- Where are the doors in every location you frequent during your day?

Examine the Hiding Places

- Under or behind your desk?
- Behind that wrestling mat?
- Inside the janitor's closet?
- Behind the kitchen freezer?

Examine the Campus Grounds

It's important that we don't get locked into thinking that a school shooting always happens inside the structure.

- In Jonesboro, Arkansas, the two shooters picked off their victims as they exited the school.
- Shooters Eric Harris and Dylan Klebold set off an explosive outside Columbine High School as a diversionary tactic. Then they set two bombs inside the cafeteria, large enough to kill virtually everyone inside and even bring down the ceiling, and moved to the parking lot to pick off fleeing students as they ran from the explosion. When the bombs didn't detonate, they shot students outside before they went on their bloody rampage inside.

- In Midland, Michigan, a 17-year-old teen shot his girlfriend four times in the parking lot.
- While working on this book, two students were shot in the mouth in the parking lot of a Catholic school in Phoenix, Arizona.

Cover and Concealment: The Difference

Cover prevents the shooter from seeing you but, more importantly, provides a shield against bullets, fire, and explosions. The following are examples of school campus cover:

- Cement walls
- Heavy cabinets
- Heavy metal desks
- Solid metal doors
- Copy machine
- Large reams of paper
- Shop machines
- Large trees
- Cafeteria freezers and stoves
- Car or truck engine blocks

Concealment is anything that prevents the shooter from seeing you, but it doesn't protect you from bullets, fire, and explosions. The following are examples of concealement:

- Hollow walls
- Hollow doors
- Teachers' desks
- Podiums
- Empty boxes
- Portable partitions
- Chalkboards
- Painted or shaded windows

- A man spent two hours in his vehicle in two parking lots of the Platte Canyon High School in Bailey, Colorado, before he walked inside, took hostages, and shot one 16-year-old girl to death.

Stand in various places outside and view the places as potential battlegrounds. If gunshots erupted from your right, where would you go? If you saw someone with a gun getting out of that red pickup, what would you do? If you heard gunshots outside but you couldn't tell from which direction, what would you do?

Virtually no innovative thinking occurs under combat conditions. Think about this now when all is calm and quiet.

Examine Common Objects as Potential Weapons
In Chapter 6 you'll find a list of improvised weapons found in most schools. For now, know that at any given time you are surrounded by weapons, but only if you can see beyond each object's original purpose. One way to see an object as a potential weapon is to play the "You know what really hurts?" game. If you're uncomfortable saying these things out loud with a friend, just think them to yourself:

- You know what really hurts? That stapler slammed into your eye.
- You know what really hurts? The janitor's bucket smashed against your head.
- You know what really hurts? This printer slammed down on your hand.

Look at the commonplace objects in your environment from the perspective of this game and it's as if you are suddenly surrounded by an arsenal.

Examine Your Environment for a Barricade

Many students and teachers in school shooting incidents have survived by barricading themselves so that the shooter was unable to reach them. Look at your school and ask how and where you would barricade yourself in your classroom. If you have more than one classroom, analyze all of them. How about the restroom? The janitor's closet? The gym storage area? The cafeteria? Can you scoot your large file cabinet over to the door? Can you squeeze behind that vending machine outside the cafeteria?

Don't wait until violence explodes—you need to know the answers to these questions now. Look around you when you're calm and collected, and determine how you can improvise given where you are in your environment and where the shooter might be located. (More on barricades later.)

Examine the Likelihood You Will Have Backup

Later sections will go into more detail on actually confronting a shooter. For now, think about your classmates and teachers:

- Is there at least one person who would help you physically confront the shooter?
- Can you talk confidentially with that person right now about your concerns about a specific person?
- If you know you would get help, how does that affect your response?
- If you know there is no one to help you, how does that affect your response?

Examine a Specific Situation

Since history tells us that violence can happen anywhere on a school campus, you want to consider every location as a potential battleground. When there is a specific person you're concerned about, you want to consider those places most frequented by him or her. However, don't focus so hard on those areas that you fail to consider other places. Remember, there are no absolutes when dealing with irrational people.

ALARM SYSTEMS

Every school in the United States has a fire alarm and practices fire alarm drills. However, how many have an alarm to warn students and staff that there is a dangerous person or persons on campus? We know that some do. The shooting that occurred at the Success Tech Academy in Cleveland while I was working on this book used an alarm system they called "Code Blue" that sent students running to find a hiding place. But since a school shooting can occur anywhere, it just makes sense that every campus has some kind of a warning system.

Why Not Just Use the Fire Alarm?

In the Jonesboro, Arkansas, middle school shooting, one of the shooters activated the fire alarm and then ran back outside to join his accomplice to wait for the kids, who thought it was a drill, to stream out the doors. But it wasn't a fire drill; it was an ambush. Two young girls held hands and sang as they walked outside, only to be shot dead by 13-year-old Mitchell Johnson and Andrew Golden, then 11. When the teachers saw what was happening, they frantically tried to herd the screaming kids back into the school, but the shooters continued firing, killing one of the staff and two more students. Before it was over, nine other students and another teacher would be shot.

Conditioned from years of fire drills, we exit the building when the alarm sounds. However, as seen from the examples just given of an active shooter, a fire alarm just might send teachers and students outside into a kill zone.

Examples of Alarm Systems

Here are some simple alarm systems that schools are using now:

Color Code
A color code system informs students and staff that there is a shooter on or in the campus. Some use "Code Blue" and others use "Code Red." Perhaps it would be best if it were universal among all schools, but until it is, or until it's shown that that isn't a good idea, any color will do as long as everyone in the school knows what it means.

Someone notifies the front office that there is an armed person on campus. The principal or a designee then calls a "Code Red" over the PA system, or whatever predesignated color is to be used. If the school doesn't have a PA system, staff and students can simply call out "Code Red!" down the hall and into the classrooms.

Code Word
The principal or a designee calls out a predetermined code word over the PA system.

Bell Alarm
The school uses a building-wide audible alarm (bells) that is distinct from the regular fire alarm sound.

Phone Tree
Teachers and office staff employ an interoffice phone tree to warn that a dangerous situation exists on campus.

Personal Alarm System
Teachers and staff carry with them a personal aerosol alarm (a hand-held device that emits a loud shriek) to set off in the event of great danger.

Familiarity with the Alarm System
Whatever system is used, it's imperative that teachers and staff know what it is and can recognize it in an instant. One simple way to do this is to spend a minute or two demonstrating it, say, once a

month, at one of the after-school staff meetings. The meeting leader says something like, "Just to remind everyone, Code Blue is our warning system that informs everyone to immediately go into a classroom, lock the doors, pull the curtains, and remain there until we issue an all-clear. So it sounds like this:"

Then someone in the office speaks into the PA system, "Code Blue! Code Blue!"

Use this simple demonstration to rehearse the bell system, personal alarm system, and code word.

Practice the phone tree anytime. The front office calls the first room and says, "This is a practice phone tree drill." The person answering that phone then calls the next room on a predesignated list. If the office has the technology to call all phones at once with a recorded warning message, that too should be rehearsed once a month.

All of these rehearsal variations take no longer than 60 seconds. Will people joke about it and have fun? Sure, and that is OK. The bottom line is to ingrain the alarm system into everyone's mind.

LOCKDOWN

The police or the principal can call for a lockdown when it's deemed that a situation is such that it's better to lock the students inside the school building than evacuate them out into a possible danger zone. The police have used lockdowns for many years when responding to a dangerous situation in a neighborhood, such as a man with a gun or an escaped convict on foot and fleeing apprehension. Officers ask their dispatch to inform the principals at nearby schools about what is occurring in the neighborhood and ask that the campuses lock down until the situation ends.

A lockdown means that everyone is locked into their rooms, and no one enters or leaves the building without permission.

In today's climate of school shootings, gang violence, and armed kids in general, the school lockdown procedure has come into the limelight more than ever. (It is useful for other dangerous situations, too. One Canadian school went into lockdown when there was a report of several pit bulls loose in the neighborhood.)

In the case of a school shooter, previous incidents show that when intruders find a locked door, they move onto the next one. They take the path of least resistance and look for easy access.

Here is how a lockdown works. Procedures change depending on the specifics of the event:

- The principal or a designated person announces the lockdown via a PA system, phone tree, a specific bell ring, or a "Code Blue" call.
- Students and staff go to the nearest classroom. All hallways are cleared, doors are closed and locked, and students and staff who are outside proceed to the gym or the closest room.
- The principal or other administrators talk to the police and decide the best action.
- Teachers keep their students calm in their locked classrooms. They move them away from the windows and doors and shut off the lights. They might tell them to lie on the floor, get under their desks, and take cover behind cabinets.

These steps need to be practiced. One principal said that they are not trying to frighten kids by practicing lockdown drills, but to make it a positive experience, a learning one. "If not practiced," he said, "there can be a lot of errors." And errors can be deadly.

Critics of Lockdown Drills

Those parents who don't like the idea of lockdown drills argue that it's frightening to children and instills a climate of fear. They further argue that in the event of a real shooting situation, all will be chaos. It's this writer's opinion that these are poor arguments, even dangerous ones:

- Fire drills don't frighten children and most schools hold them monthly. In those schools that conduct lockdown drills once or twice a year, teachers read to the younger children to distract them and keep them calm.
- Because young children learn from the first day of school to form lines, walk together from one room to another, and to sit in designated places, they are more likely than older students to do the right thing in a real lockdown event.
- Those parents who don't want it because they think that all will be chaos in a real situation need to understand that a trained response is more likely to save their children's lives and less likely to cause them to respond in panic.
- One woman who was running for a school board position in Canada stated, "I still have questions about why we are doing this. I still think it's done in the interests of police and lawyers. It's not in the interests of kids. I want children to feel that school is a safe place not likely to be invaded by armed men." One wonders if this naïve woman is comfortable with fire drills, though there have been far more incidents of school shootings than school fires.

During my long law enforcement career, it was always a personal battle in frustration for me to try to get people who have never experienced one iota of personal tragedy, violence, or danger to believe that these things really exist. Some people were in profound denial or, to be frank, were as dumb as a breadbox. Even more frustrating was when such a person was in a position of influence, such as a mayor, school board member, teacher, or principal.

As I worked on this book, talking with people and researching information, I quickly discovered that there are still people in denial even after so many school massacres. I'd ask them, "Does your kid's school have a plan in place should a shooter come onto campus?"

More times than not, I got a shrug. "I don't know. Maybe I should ask."

Gee, ya think?

Parents have a responsibility to keep their schools on task and schools have a responsibility and a liability to keep children safe. If a school shooter goes on a rampage through the halls and the only response by staff and students is to panic, the lawsuits are going to be biblical in proportion. "You did nothing to prevent my child from getting shot," parents will charge. "In light of what's been happening on school campuses, why didn't you prepare for this?"

Those who fail in their responsibility to protect our children's safety will have to contend with years of lawsuits—and a lifetime of guilt.

Police officers, soldiers, and hospital emergency room staff all know the importance of training and rehearsal. A practiced response will beget a smoother response in reality. If students and teachers never practice a response or deny that they will ever need to know what to do, a real situation just might overwhelm them.

We will look at lockdown specifics later.

METAL DETECTORS

While there are schools that have walk-through metal detectors and metal detecting wands, not everyone agrees that they are a solution. One pundit wondered what good they are when a determined shooter will simply gun down the people working them. After all, school shooters have gunned down armed security officers. Another critic argued that schools should focus more on listening to students, investigating threats, and working to uncover plots. Another said that they lead to false confidence, citing the Red Lake High School massacre in Minnesota where the student shooter still killed seven people on the campus in spite of its metal detectors.

Those in favor argue that a metal detector is worth the expense if it stops one kid from bringing a weapon to school, prevents one person from getting shot or stabbed, and reduces fear and anxiety among students and staff.

One study done in New York City high schools found that kids who attended schools with metal detectors were half as likely to carry a gun, knife, or other weapon to or from school or inside the building, as were students who attended schools without metal detectors.

My thinking is that when kids have to pass through metal detectors beginning in kindergarten, then in elementary, middle, and high school, the simple process will just be part of their day. Metal detectors will be no more traumatizing than having to pass through those at the airport or hearing the sudden clanging of a fire alarm that sends everyone outside. We warn kids about strangers and drugs—implying that both will do something terrible to them—without it devastating their psyches, so can walking through a metal detecting doorway cause them harm?

There are those who argue that getting scanned violates kids' rights, that "it sends the wrong message," and that the situation "isn't that bad." These people need to sit down face-to-face and express their opinions with the survivors of Columbine and Virginia Tech, and with hundreds of other students and teachers who have been under the gun, been bloodied, and watched innocent life drain from young people who only moments before had their entire lives before them. Then they need to argue their points to the parents of the dozens and dozens of kids who have fallen dead before the guns of mentally deranged shooters who had only to stroll easily and unchecked into a school where, without resistance, they transformed its halls into killing grounds.

THE CHALLENGE OF UNDERSTANDING
VIOLENT REALITY

There is no way that words can convey the sights, sounds, and smells of the horror of a teenager wantonly discharging a firearm into the bodies of his classmates. A creative movie director and a special effects expert can duplicate the roar of gunshots and the terrified screams of victims in the hallways and classrooms. But they cannot reproduce the terrible feeling of your heart slamming into your throat, fear's acidic taste, muscles refusing to support your body, blindness from excessive tearing, and the gut-twisting sense of doom.

Parents, teachers, staff, and mature high school students need to understand the contents of this chapter. Parents should talk with their high school kids about it. I leave it to parents of grade school children as to how best to address some of these frightening issues.

In recent years, our police agencies and military have incorporated more and more realistic training—blaring sound, strobing lights, smoke, explosions, and nonlethal, welt-producing bullets—that helps duplicate the adrenaline rush and accelerated heart rate of battle. But while they cannot achieve total realism, these warriors are benefiting from the training in such a way that today they are functioning at a greater level in real deadly situations than ever before.

What about your child? Although you can't send him through Army Special Forces combat training or your local police SWAT training, you can strive to make your older child understand that a real situation isn't a bloody Quentin Tarantino movie. It might look like it a little, but even the famed director of violent film can't duplicate the powerful psychological and physiological effects on your child's mind and body that can affect how he reacts and how he thinks.

Since your child has never experienced these things, he might not believe they will happen to him. Of course, arguing is what a kid does, but don't let that stop you from talking to him about the reality of such an event. Then should he get into a real situation and these feelings and thoughts slam into him like a Mack truck, he is more likely to remember what you told him. Remembering what you said helps your child understand that what he is experiencing is perfectly normal in an abnormal situation. With that understanding, he can function and do what he has to do to save himself, and perhaps others.

As an older student or a teacher who has read this book, practiced the lessons and thought deeply about what you would do should such horror come to your campus, you are at a far greater advantage than those who are living in denial that it would ever happen.

The interested reader wanting a complete examination of the toxic impact of sudden violence on one's mind and body should see my books, *Deadly Force Encounters*, coauthored with Dr. Alexis Artwohl, and *On Combat: The Psychology and Physiology of Deadly Conflict in War and in Peace*, coauthored with Lt. Col. Dave Grossman. Both are available through Paladin Press.

Same Violence, Different Schools

Examine any number of school shooting incidents and you find that while the people and the places are different, the senselessness, explosiveness, bedlam, shock, and horror are the same. New theaters, new actors, same deadly third acts.

- In Westmount, Canada, a 25-year-old man brought a carbine, a Glock 9mm pistol, and a shotgun to Dawson College and began firing outside the school entrance. He proceeded into the school and toward the atrium next to the cafeteria. Before the morning ended, 19 people would be wounded, one person would die and, after being wounded by the police, the shooter would kill himself.
- In Emsdetten, Germany, an 18-year-old walked into his old alma mater armed with explosives and two sawed-off shotguns. He would injure nine students, one teacher, 16 police officers, and a janitor before killing himself.
- In Cold Spring, Minnesota, a 15-year-old boy brought a handgun to school with the intention of shooting another student who he later said had been teasing him. The gunman confronted his target in a basement hallway and fired twice, the first round hitting the student, the second missing but hitting another person. Both victims would die from their injuries. A teacher apprehended the shooter.
- In Blacksburg, Virginia, a mentally ill Virginia Tech student went on a shooting rampage, firing 174 rounds, killing 32, wounding at least 17 more. After he killed himself, investigators found two knives, a claw hammer, and 203 additional rounds on his body, a clear indication that the shooting could have been far worse.
- In Bemidji, Minnesota, a high school student, armed with two handguns and a shotgun, began his day of shooting by gunning down his grandparents at his home. From there he went to his school where he shot a security guard, and then proceeded down a hallway and into a classroom where he shot a teacher and several students. Before the morning would end, he would wound 15 people, kill seven, and then kill himself after exchanging gunfire with police.

Bedlam

School campuses are not quiet, sedate places. To the contrary, the atmosphere is a charged one, as kids shout, laugh, slam lockers, dribble balls, and call out friends' names, all with a palpable electric energy typical of school settings everywhere. Gunfire in this setting is so alien, so unacceptable to the brain that it's denied—at first.

Is that the janitor beating on pipes? Did some kids bring fireworks to school? Heads peer around hallway corners and out classroom door windows. A splatter of nervous laugher from somewhere. A louder bang reverberates off the walls. Wide-eyed faces look at each other questioningly. Then another bang, and another. Acceptance hits like an artillery round. Cries of *"Oh my God!"*

Then absolute chaos.

Here are some actual quotes from students who survived school shootings:

"Everyone was yelling, 'Get in the gym! Get in the gym!' At first we thought it was a fight. Then the teachers started getting on the tables and screaming." —Sam Sao, 14 [2]

"I heard five shots go off, and I saw glass shattering all over the front office, and then I saw all my principals get down on the ground." —Jake Lowe, a junior [3]

"I heard like firecrackers. People were running and screaming. There were two bodies and blood was everywhere." —Student (declined to give name to reporters) [4]

"I was probably 10 feet away from some of the victims . . . I saw a boy laying on the floor with his face downward. Everybody was running. A whole lot of people were crying. Nobody knew what really happened. . . . Then all of a sudden we heard more shots going off. It sounded more like a cap gun than anything. It was really scary." —Alicia Zimmer, student (age and grade unknown)[5]

Although the shooter often hints at his plan by what he tells others or writes in notebooks, letters, or in an online blog, the actual event is still perceived as sudden, explosive, and mind boggling to everyone on the scene. Generally, the shooter walks up to the first victim—sometimes the intended one, sometimes a random one—and fires a bullet into his body. If there are others in the immediate area, they might pause for as long as it takes their brains to catch up to the surreal happening. It's a pause that is often fatal.

Then comes the screaming and shouting, and you're caught smack in the middle of it.

Confusion: Kids and teachers running in front of you, running behind you, slamming into you, knocking you down. *Got to get up. Got to run. Which way should I go? There he is! Oh my God, there he is! I thought he was around the corner.*

Sounds: the principal shouting, people screaming, curses, doors slamming, a trashcan rolling down the hall, someone shouting an incoherent warning. *Is that moaning? From where?* Feet running. *Was that another shot? Yes. Several of them. The echo . . . can't tell what direction it's coming from. My heart thumping so hard. Can't breathe. Eyes watering. Can't see.* Another shot, louder

Sometimes the Shooter Has a Plan

The killer comes to school looking for one person to shoot. Such was the case with a shooter in Paducah, Kentucky, who opened fire on a prayer group. Likewise with a shooter in Midland, Michigan, who shot his ex-girlfriend. But these shooters didn't stop there: They continued to kill.

Sometimes they have a specific strategy, like the Virginia Tech shooter who first chained the front doors shut to trap the victims inside, and like the two shooters in Jonesboro, Arkansas ,who first pulled the fire alarm and then took up position in a field where they shot students as they exited the building.

than before. *Is he shooting at me?* Crying. Lots of crying every-where. There's a body on the stairs. *It's so . . . still. So. Very. Still. What should I do? Is he coming into my classroom? People run-ning outside the door. Shots! So close! Someone is pushing on the door. Got to find cover. Got to hide. There he is! It's too late. I . . . can't . . . move.*

WHAT HAPPENS TO YOUR MIND AND BODY UNDER GREAT STRESS

Even police officers—people generally better trained to handle high-risk situations than average citizens, and who get at least annual training in how to function in violent confrontations—can still be affected negatively by sudden, explosive violence. Officers training with Simunition (a type of live, nonlethal ammunition that leaves a painful welt on the trainees' skin) have recorded heart rates in excess of 225 beats per minute (bpm). Imagine the bpm of an average school student and teacher who have never experienced the harsh reality of sudden violence.

Let's look at why a stress-induced heart rate isn't a good thing.

Your Heart Rate

Somewhere in the area of 175 bpm, your ability to function deteriorates (a teenager's normal resting heart rate is between 60 and 100 bpm), the exception being those police officers and sol-diers who have learned to work in this realm. But if you haven't trained to think clearly and strategically and perform fine-motor skills with such an accelerated heart rate, most likely your per-formance will suffer, if you can perform at all.

Now, you might argue that you consistently push your heart rate to 175 bpm when jogging or pumping on the Stairmaster and that afterward, you can perform fine-motor skills, such as setting the time on your watch or inserting your car key into a door. That is because an accelerated heart rate from exercise isn't the same as an accelerated heart rate caused by fear and a desperate need to survive.

The mirror reveals the difference:

An accelerated heart rate caused by exercise flushes your face (turns it red, if you're light skinned) as blood vessels dilate to allow blood to surge to your muscles.

An accelerated heart rate caused by fear pales your face (turns it white, if you're light skinned) because of vasoconstriction, the narrowing of blood vessels that constricts or slows blood flow.

Should you run in desperation, adding physical exertion to your panic, your body will require additional fresh, oxygenated blood, just as your fear-induced vasoconstriction shuts down or constricts the vessels that deliver this much-needed supply. The result: an even higher heart rate.

Your heart rate can go from 70 bpm to 220 bpm in less than half a second.

Let's take a quick look at the stages of an accelerated heart rate, data based on an article by researchers Bruce Siddle and Dr. Hal Breedlove entitled "Survival Stress Reaction" and from Siddle's excellent book *Sharpening the Warrior's Edge: The Psychology and Science of Training.* When we talk about fear-induced accelerated heart rate, we're talking about Survival Stress Reaction (SSR):

- Around 115 bpm, most people lose fine motor skills, such as finger dexterity and eye-hand coordination, making it virtually impossible to, say, type in a code to unlock a door, work a combination lock, or find the right key in a cluster of keys.

Multitasking also becomes difficult.

- Around 145 bpm, most people lose their complex motor skills, movements that involve a series of muscle groups, such as eye-hand coordination, precise tracking of movement, and exact timing. Executing complicated self-defense techniques becomes difficult.
- Around 175 bpm, most people experience numerous negative effects: tunnel vision (meaning a loss of depth perception) and loss of memory of what happened (though there is usually a 30 percent recall after the first 24 hours, 50 percent after two days, and 75 to 95 percent after three to four days).
- At 185–220 bpm, most people go into a state of "hypervigilance," sometimes referred to as the "deer in the headlights" mode. This is often characterized by performing actions that are useless, such as continuing to desperately twist a doorknob on a locked door. People in this condition are often unable to move or scream. When they do move, they sometimes do so irrationally by leaving their place of cover.

Always refer to the emergency number as "nine-one-one," not "nine-eleven." Under stress your child—even some adults—will hunt for the eleven on the phone.

Trained people have an advantage. Your SSR, whether it's in the 115 bpm range or 220, happens without conscious thought. Siddle and other researchers of SSR tested police officers and soldiers, people in high-risk jobs who engage in considerable training that is far greater in quantity and sophistication than what the average person gets. Their research has found that a trained person can function with an accelerated heart rate of 115 to 145 bpm, and when it climbs higher, a trained person can lower it consciously to within that workable area.

WHAT CAN YOU DO?

In a perfect world, teachers, staff, and students would get some aspects of the training given to police departments and the military. However, most school districts can't afford the time or the cost, not to mention the problems that would most likely arise among the participants: lack of fitness, disabilities, age limitations, lack of motivation, grievances, and a host of other issues. Then there is the field day the media would have with it.

But not all is bleak. There are some things you can do ahead of time to minimize your SSR to some degree, steps that increase your confidence and even your physical ability to respond. By putting into practice the training ideas suggested in the following pages, you will be far ahead of those who bury their heads in the sand and pretend that nothing bad will ever happen.

The first skill to learn and practice is that of breathing (the second being mentl imagery). Yes, you already have that one down, but this is a powerful method that will amaze you with its incredible ability to bring on physical and mental calm within seconds.

Four-Count Combat Breathing

Four-count breathing is a highly effective and easy-to-do technique that slows your thumping heartbeat, reduces the tremble in your hands, clears your mind, and envelops you in a sense of calm and control. Though this powerful tool has been used in the martial arts, yoga, and medical field for a long time, in recent years it has been popularized in the military and law enforcement communities by Lt. Col. Dave Grossman and others. He and I coauthored *On Combat,* from which this procedure and some of the aforementioned heart rate data was taken.

The technical term for the procedure is autogenic breathing, but police officers and soldiers call it tactical breathing or combat breathing. Many SWAT officers use it just before they make forced entry into a drug house where there are armed and dangerous subjects. Soldiers use it to bring calm to their minds and bodies before they go into battle and then again after the battle to "come down" from the adrenaline rush. High school and college students are finding that it reduces test anxiety, and many surgeons are using it before beginning a delicate operating procedure where optimum fine-motor control is needed.

How to Do It

Begin by breathing in through your nose to a slow count of four, feeling your lower belly expand. Hold for a slow count of four, and then slowly exhale through your lips for a count of four, letting your belly deflate. Hold empty for a slow count of four and then repeat the process. Here is the entire procedure:

* Breathe in through the nose two, three, four. Hold two, three, four.
* Exhale out through the lips two, three, four. Hold two, three, four.
* Breathe in through the nose deep, deep, deep. Hold two, three, four.
* Exhale out through the lips. Hold two, three, four.
* Breathe in through the nose two, three, four. Hold two, three, four.
* Exhale out through the lips two, three, four. Hold two, three, four.

That's it. Simple. You don't need to sit before a candle or burn incense. It can be done anywhere, anytime. Read on.

Combat Breathing in Action

In *Surviving Workplace Violence*, I tell of using combat breathing once when I made a bad decision as a police officer and found myself alone and jostled between two opposing groups of protestors. Even while being threatened by both sides and while being pressed against a door, I began to do 4-count combat breathing, quietly and invisibly. Within seconds, my shakes and quivering stopped, and my eyes stopped watering so that I was able to think clearly and take command of the situation.

I also used it as a police officer during those seconds just before we "keyed a door" (smashed through it with a 40-pound steel ram) on a drug raid, and I even used it when driving fast to a violent call. These days I use it to bring a sense of calm when life throws 20 things at me at once.

Teachers and Older Students: Tailor It to Your Needs

The beauty of this wonderful tool is that you can adapt it easily to your needs. While most people find that the described three-cycle procedure works well to bring calm to their minds and bodies, you might need four to six cycles to get the benefits. You might also prefer to hold each count for five seconds rather than four. That's fine. It's about making it work for you. But don't wait until you're in the middle of a dangerous situation to experiment. Practice this breathing procedure once or twice a day to learn what method works best for you (and to award yourself with a few moments of calm and clarity). Practice now so that it will be there for you when you need it most.

Parents: Teach this Variation to Your Young Kids

This is a wonderful technique that some teachers use to calm their six-year-olds after recess. It teaches kids to use their hands to follow their breathing, which makes the technique fun for them and easy to remember. Here is how you can combine this effective tool with four-count breathing. Since it might be hard for them to count and breathe at the same time, you do it for them, ensuring that each phase is four seconds long:

- Your child sits in a chair or on the floor cross-legged and, with slightly bent arms, holds his open hands in front of him about chest high, the little finger sides of his hands touching, as if holding a flat plate.

- As he breathes in slowly, he slowly lifts his palms as high as his chin. (4 seconds)
- He slowly turns his hands over so that the thumbs sides are touching. (4 seconds)
- As he exhales slowly, he slowly lowers his palms to chest height. (4 seconds)
- He slowly turns his hands over so that the little finger sides are touching. (4 seconds)

That is one cycle. Teach him to do three. Be sure to make it a fun activity.

Then after they can do it smoothly—it might take a few days of practice—put it to practical use. Use it to calm a wound-up kid before bedtime or use it when he awakens from a dream frightened. Use it to calm your child after he comes in the house from rambunctious play or when he gets angry at a sibling. Always do it with him and then, after the third cycle (it's OK to do four or five cycles if he will sit still for it), say something like, "Wow. I sure feel relaxed now. Don't you?" You might even let him see you do it a few times by yourself.

Once this becomes routine—it might take a week or two—mention to your child that he can do it whenever he gets upset. He can even do it at school if something really bothers him or something scary happens.

Teachers: Teach It to Your Students

As mentioned, many teachers use the combination hand motion and breathing to calm their charges after a rambunctious recess or gym class. But you can use it anytime you want to bring calm to your kids. The more often you use it, the more they see how it helps quiet and calm the class. It's important that you articulate to them what they're doing and why. "OK, class. Let's all do our calm breathing. Hands up, ready and inhale, one, two . . ." This helps them associate the word "calm" with the effect they get and with their action. Then end the brief session with, "Thank you class. Remember, you can do calm breathing anytime you feel yourself get nervous or scared." Imprint this in their minds so that it's there for them when they need it most.

Mental Imagery: For Teachers and Older Students

Today, virtually all Olympic athletes include mental imagery in their training, as they consider it a powerful and vital tool that prepares them for the stress of high-caliber competition. More and more high school and college athletes are using it, too, as are professionals and amateurs in every area of competition. The broad acceptance of mental imagery in sport has lead to it becoming increasingly commonplace in police work and the military where officers and soldiers need to prepare in detail for every eventuality.

What Is Mental Imagery?

Mental imagery is a simple but powerful tool to rehearse an effective response to a violent encounter on your campus. Should you work or attend a school in which students and staff physically practice a response to shooting in progress, you can still practice this technique to solidify what you have learned. However, if your school is like most in that you practice fire drills but not violent incident drills (a monumental lawsuit will change that), mental imagery is one way that you can take charge of how you will react.

The beauty of this practice is that you can do it in your easy chair at home, in your car while waiting for someone, or just anytime you have a few moments to engage in quiet contemplation. The technique is simple, although there is a series of complex processes occurring in your mind and body that controlled studies have shown provides nearly the same benefits as does physically practicing an action. Think of it as a mental rehearsal that might very well mean the difference between confusion and relatively clear thinking, between freezing and acting to save yourself and the lives of others, and between confidence in knowing that you have a plan of action instead of thinking that you're helpless at the hands of an attacker.

How Is it Done?

Although you will eventually be able to practice just about anywhere and anytime, find a quiet and comfortable place for the first few practice sessions, and settle in. Use the four-count breathing technique discussed earlier to bring calm and relaxation to your mind and body. The more tranquil you are, the more receptive you will be to your conjured images.

The scenario: You're a teacher or student in a classroom when you hear three distinct gunshots from out in the hall, followed by several screams.

Should you use first person or third person viewing? Some people imagine seeing everything unfold through their eyes, which is called "first person viewing," while others see themselves as if watching a character on a movie screen, often called "third person viewing." Roughly one-third of top athletes and firearms shooters see their activity unfold out of their eyes, roughly a third use the third person method, and the last third use both. Try them all and see if you have a preference. If you don't, use both methods depending how you feel that day. Studies show that both are effective.

You must employ all of your senses to achieve optimum benefit from your practice:

- *See* your environment: the chalkboards, chairs, students, desks, and wall maps. See where you are in the room, see what is near you, and see what is across the room.
- *Hear* running steps from out in the hall, followed by screams

and the sound of two gunshots from farther down the hall. Hear the students around you shout and cry out. Hear their chairs scoot on the floor.

- *Smell* the usual odors associated with a classroom: chalk, glue, and old books. Then smell the odor of gun smoke wafting through the door.
- *Taste* the acrid cloud of gun smoke.
- *Feel* your heart race, feel someone brush by you as they race to the door. Feel the confidence you have gained from having studied your campus and your classroom, from having paid attention to suspicious people in the school, from having discussed a proper response with a close friend, and from having practiced mental imagery to rehearse your actions.

Bring these sensory elements to your mental imagery each time you practice. Make it real so that your mind and body benefit from your imagined experience.

See all the action at the same speed in which it would actually happen. If it would take you 10 seconds to run from the front of the room to behind a cabinet at the back of the room, imagine it happening at that speed. This means you can mentally practice four or five times in a minute, up to 20 times in five minutes.

Let's continue. You hear screams and shots from out in the hall, you smell gun smoke, you see and hear students in your classroom leaping to their feet and beginning to panic. Consider the following ideas as to how to respond. They will vary depending on your environment and the scenario you imagine, and whether you're a teacher or older student:

- *See* yourself rush toward the door as you gesture to the others to move to the rear of the classroom.
- *Feel* your hand grasp the door and shut it quickly, but quietly. Feel your fingers grasp the door handle lock and turn it to secure the door. *See* and *feel* your hands reach for the light switch and turn the lights off. *Feel* your hand pull down the curtain and, just before it gets all the way down, *see* a kid at the other end of the hall around the corner, a rifle of some kind in each hand.
- *Feel* your pulse and breathing quicken.
- *See* yourself gesturing for two big kids to help you push the teacher's desk over to block the door. *See* yourself waving your hands so the students can see you. *See* yourself put a finger to your lips for them to be quiet and then pantomime someone holding a rifle. *See* yourself point toward the door so they know what you mean.
- *See* and *feel* yourself and the other two people push that desk quickly and quietly up against the door.

The doors in most schools open out into the hall. Although you can't barricade the doors shut from inside, blocking the doorway with desks, bookcases, and other large objects just might discourage the shooter so that he moves on to another location or slows him down enough for you to escape out a window.

- *See* yourself move quickly toward the back of the classroom with the others as you pantomime a person holding a rifle. *See* yourself point toward the door to indicate that person is out in the hall and then gesture for everyone to get down on the floor.
- *Hear* another shot from out in the hall. *Hear* more running footsteps. *Hear* another scream.

- *Feel* yourself hug the floor and hold the hand of a student lying next to you.
- *Feel* your heart rate and breathing accelerate.
- *See* desperate faces look at you. *See* your finger move to your lips to encourage everyone to keep quiet.
- *Hear* the doorknob rattle from out in the hall. *Hear* students whimpering.
- *See* yourself again encouraging them to be quiet.
- *Feel* yourself begin to do 4-count breathing to keep yourself calm.
- *See* the doorknob stop turning.
- *Hear* footsteps outside the door walk away.

With these added elements, your imagined scenario might take 30 seconds, which means you can get in several repetitions within five minutes. As mentioned, you should initially practice in a quiet place, but once you're comfortable with the process, you can do it anywhere and no one needs to know.

Be Creative

Use your imagery to create all kinds of scenarios. The more you use your imagination, the more detail you bring to your mental imagery, the more likely you will react with experience in a real situation.

Move a Little

While mental imagery is done in your mind, you don't have to always sit perfectly still when practicing. Just as you want to include all your senses, you should also practice from time to time using mini-movements that mimic what you're imaging. You're not moving at full speed, full force, or with full extension of your limbs, but simply using small, gentle movements to give you a sense of "feel" with your imagery.

Say you want to practice dashing from your desk to the classroom door, pushing it shut, locking it, and pulling down the window curtain. Here is how you would practice this 10-second action:

- *Sit* in a comfortable chair and bring on a sense of relaxation using the 4-count breathing technique.
- *See* yourself sitting at your desk in the classroom and hear the screams and gunshots from out in the hall. Physically turn your head and body two or three inches as if reacting to the uproar.
- *Feel* the energy in your legs as you begin to see yourself stand up quickly. Physically push off your feet a couple of inches to mimic the action of getting up, though you don't actually do it.
- *Feel* and *see* your upper body lean forward a little as if you were scurrying across the room toward the door. Physically lean forward.
- *See* and *feel* your hands reach forward a couple of inches as if reaching toward the open door. Physically reach forward.
- *See* and *feel* your palms extend forward a couple of inches to push the door quietly closed. Physically push your hands forward.
- *See* and *feel* your right hand twist a little as if turning the lock. Physically twist your hand, configuring it to grip whatever kind of mechanism your door has.
- *See* and *feel* your left hand reach up a couple of inches as if clasping the curtain rope and see and feel your hand descend a little as if pulling the curtain down to cover the window. Physically mimic the motion.
- *See* and *feel* your body turn a couple of inches as you imagine yourself turning to run toward the back of the room. Physically turn a little.

How Effective Is Mental Imagery?

How much better will your response be in a real situation after you have trained with mental imagery? It's impossible to know for sure because there are so many variables in any situation. But controlled studies and anecdotal reports from top athletes, law enforcement officers, soldiers and martial artists show that mental imagery practice works, and works well.

There is nothing mystical about it, while at times the incredible results might make it seem so. Think of it as a rehearsal like those fire drills you physically practice, only much more effective.

We look more into mental imagery later when we examine how you can fight back when you have no other options.

ENDNOTES

1. "Student kills 2 classmates, wounds 13 near San Diego." CNN online. http://archives.cnn.com/2001/US/03/05/school.shooting.05/ index.html. Posted March 5, 2001. Accessed July 10, 2008.

2. "Student arrested after shooting of teenager in school hallway." CNN online. http://www.usatoday.com/news/nation/2007-01-03-school-shooting_x.htm. Posted January 3, 2007. Accessed July 10, 2008.

3. "Five injured in teen's rampage at Granite Hills." By Jeff McDonald. *Union-Tribune.* March 23, 2001. Available online at http://www.signonsandiego.com/news/metro/granitehills/20010323-9999_1n23sklmain2.html. Accessed July 10, 2008.

4. "1 killed, 25 wounded in Oregon school shooting." CNN online. http://www.cnn.com/US/9805/21/school.shooting.2/. Posted May 21, 1998. Accessed July 10, 2008.

5. "Student kills 2 classmates, wounds 13 near San Diego." CNN online. http://archives.cnn.com/2001/US/03/05/school.shooting.05/ index.html. Posted March 5, 2001. Accessed July 10, 2008.

Chapter 5

Under Fire

*I looked out the window and there was a kid with a trench coat
and a shotgun and pipe bombs in the parking lot. And then he shot
a girl outside and then he came into the cafeteria and you could
hear, like, bombs and shotguns going off.*
                          —Unidentified girl, Columbine High School

The thought of your children "under fire" is almost too horrific to fathom. But as we have seen throughout this text, it's a sad realty that is happening repeatedly throughout the country, every school year. As uncomfortable as it might be, you must talk to your children about what they should do when a school shooter suddenly opens fire where they are.

TALKING WITH YOUR KIDS ABOUT WHAT TO DO

Many parents in denial or concerned about frightening their children refuse to address the issue of what to do. One wonders what these parents are going to say to their children after the fact, when they ask, "Why didn't you teach us what to do? Why didn't you try to protect us?"

Talking to Teens

As the parent, you're the best judge as to how to talk with *and listen to* your children. In general, those in high school and even some middle school kids are already knowledgeable about the subject, a result of seeing it on the news and talking about it in school and among friends. Don't talk to them about the lurid details of a recent school shooting, but rather let them air their feelings and concerns about it. After they have talked about theirs, let them know what you're thinking and feeling. Then talk with them about what actions they would take should something like that happen in their school. Point out the suggestions in this book, discuss them, and leave it on the kitchen table where they can peruse it on their own.

Talking to Younger Children

Don't go into great detail with young children because it will likely scare and confuse them. Don't let them watch the news when there has been such an event, as the images might frighten them and even confuse them into thinking that the incident happened at their school. Assure them that their teachers, the principal, the police, and you are working hard to keep them safe on the campus.

Here are a few ways that some parents talk to their young children about how to respond. You will notice that some are quite veiled while others are straight to the point (it's interesting to note that the latter is recommended by at least one child psychologist):

- "If you were a mouse and you were being chased by a cat,

My Kids

My three kids have all told me that they remember our kitchen table talks about what to do if a shooter came to their school or if a burglar came into the house. They remember that even when they were younger, I didn't mince words. I used terms like, "shooter," bad man," and "scary guy." They were not hurt by it and there was never any doubt in their minds what I was talking about.

---

where are places you can hide in your classroom? The library?
The cafeteria?"
- "If a mean dog got into the school, where are places you can
  hide in your classroom? The library? The cafeteria?"
- "If you were playing hide-and-go-seek, where are places you
  can hide in your classroom? The library? The cafeteria?"

The idea with the above examples is that the children will have
at least thought about places to hide. One child therapist disagreed,
arguing that kids won't be able to equate hiding for fun with hiding from someone firing a gun. She suggests being more straight-
forward because young kids know about guns and bad people from
television programs, movies, television news, and video games.
She suggests that parents say:

- "A bad guy is in your school: Where are places you can hide
  in your classroom? The library? The cafeteria?"
- "Someone scary is in your school: Where are places you can
  hide in your classroom? The library? The cafeteria?"
- "There's someone with a gun in your school: Where are places
  you can hide in your classroom? The library? The cafeteria?"

Ask your kids what they know. Kids of all ages often have
inaccurate information. Ask where they got it and, if it's
inaccurate, correct it.

There are two types of victims when a shooter comes to
school: Those who get a warning and those who don't.

YOU HAVE NO WARNING

When you're eating lunch and you hear someone shout that

someone with a gun is coming toward the cafeteria, you at least have a moment to plan, react, and take evasive action. The more you have thought in advance about this horrific moment, the faster and smoother will be your reaction.

But what about when there is no forewarning? What if you're in the first classroom the gunman enters?

Say you're a student in class listening to the teacher, or you're the teacher writing on the chalkboard when the door slams open against the wall and someone rushes in looking over a rifle like a SWAT policeman. You don't even have time to be stunned before the weapon explodes and a kid sitting in the front row launches backward off his chair and onto the floor, twitches once, and stops.

The only way out is the door where the gunman is standing. He shoots again.

You can drop to the floor and play dead, or you can run in a crouch along the wall and hope the gunman is so focused on his shots that he doesn't see you. If you play dead, you're vulnerable to him firing a round into you to make sure you're finished. Or he might think his work is done and he leaves the room. If you dash along the wall, you might be able to get behind him and attack, using any of the methods described in this book. Or your movement might draw his attention to shoot at you.

Both options carry great risk. A third option is to do nothing, except cower and be a trembling target. A fourth is to run about in total panic and confusion and be a target.

FLEE THE AREA

The killer's face is as cold as the three guns and 75 rounds of ammunition he's packing, and his eyes stare a thousand yards into another world, a place where he is sole judge and executioner. Walking up to him and saying, "Hey Tommy, can we talk?" isn't an option. Getting away from him as fast as you can is.

To run or not to run is a judgment call made when your heart is slamming against your throat as your world abruptly transforms into a place of absolute terror. This is why it's so critical that you think, plan, and visualize your actions now when you're calm and collected.

Opportunity and an Avenue of Escape

You need two elements to flee successfully: opportunity and an avenue of escape:

Opportunity: You can run when the gunman is at the far end of the cafeteria.

Avenue of escape: There is an escape route when the path to the closest door is unobstructed.

Opportunity: You can run when someone shouts that the shooter is on his way to where you are by way of the north door.

Avenue of escape: There is a place to flee to when the south door is unlocked and close to you.

An exception to the opportunity rule: Say you're face to face with the shooter and, though there is an aisle next to you that leads straight to the door 20 feet away, he says he will shoot if you move. You have an avenue of escape but not an opportunity.

Indications are that he is going to shoot you anyway. So should

Should You Try to Talk to Him?

There is no absolute answer. If you know the student, talking to him might help. It has in past shootings, although there have been many in which it didn't.

Keep in mind that the shooter's mind is likely in another place, a dark world where all he sees are targets. Anything you say or do, no matter how sound it might look on paper, just might be the very thing that sets him off even more.

you run? Yes, because maybe he is a lousy shot. No, because maybe he isn't. This dilemma is a likely possibility, one you should think about now, while your heart rate is normal and your thinking is clear.

Let's say you've decided to flee the area:

- Try to keep objects—desks, cabinets, vehicles, boxes, machinery—between you and the shooter to both obstruct his view of you and possibly absorb or deflect any bullets he sends your way.
- Don't zigzag; just run hard.
- If you can grab something to use as a weapon without slowing, do it. It might come in handy later.
- Know that a bullet can travel a mile or more. While it can be argued that you're harder to hit when a shooter aims and fires from 40 feet away (which has been recommended as a minimum distance to flee), know that a missed bullet fired at a closer target might still hit you, though you might be much farther than 40 feet away.
- If you can't get out the door, go out a window. If you can't open it, break the window with a chair or heavy object by striking the weaker, lower corner of the pane. Breaking glass makes noise, so leap through the opening and run like the wind.
- When you're able to flee from inside the school to the outside, or you're outside and the shooting is occurring outside, run behind trees, vehicles, and buildings that can block you from the shooter's view as well as stop bullets. Use your cell phone to call 9-1-1.

If you can't run, you need to hide. This is important whether the shooter is looking specifically for you, someone like you—all white people, all people of color, all athletes—or is attacking people randomly.

School shootings are explosive and fast paced. The two suspects in the Columbine shooting fired 188 shots, killing 13 people and wounding 21 in less than 49 minutes. The solo shooter at Virginia Tech fired more than 170 rounds, killing 32 people and wounding 17 in less than nine minutes.

A Word about Walls and Floors

Know that when a bullet strikes a wall or the floor at certain angles, it travels along the surface. So a bullet that hits a wall just right, say, 20 feet from a corner, will travel its length until it runs out of energy or, more likely, something stops it, like a face peering around the corner.

If you're hiding behind a car, crouch down behind a tire. If you have a choice, choose a front tire so that you're behind the engine block. Should you kneel at the middle of the car, a bullet that hits the pavement several feet away can travel along the surface under the car and into your shins.

HIDE

When considering places to hide and places to use as barricades, keep in mind that it's possible to get trapped. Say you've made a fortress and you're well hidden when a window of opportunity to escape opens. But you can't take it because you're so secreted that to make a break for it would likely give away your position before you could reach safety.

If time permits, choose a hiding place that gives you concealment and cover.

Consider this during your preplanning sessions. Ask yourself, If I hide there or barricade myself behind that, can I get out quickly given an opportunity? For example, a typical restroom might seem like a good hiding place but could become a trap if there's only one way out. If there's no safe way to get out, consider another place. If you can't find one, you have to go with the first and hope for the best:

Gym
- Under a stack of wrestling mats
- Inside a bin of basketballs
- Inside a shower stall
- Under a pile of towels
- Inside a storage room
- Inside a crawl space
- Inside a ceiling opening
- Inside a cabinet

The Irony of Hiding Places

The same places where you can hide are also places where the shooter can hide as he waits for the right moment to begin his violent rampage. This is why it's important that you remain in Condition Yellow from the moment you leave home at the beginning of your day until you return home at its end. Be especially alert to hiding places at or near the entry to your school:

- Large shrubbery and trees
- Dumpsters
- Vehicles
- Breezeways
- Adjacent buildings
- Landscape configurations: large stones, mounds, ponds, signs

Office Area
- Under or behind desks
- Behind cabinets, copy machines, desks, storage cabinets, large potted plants, or partitions
- In the ceiling (remove a ceiling tile, hoist yourself up and into the opening, then replace the tile)
- Break rooms (a cupboard large enough to squeeze inside or behind the door)
- Restrooms (inside a stall with both feet up on the toilet)
- Coat closets, maintenance closets, and small storage areas

Playing Fields, Parking Lots, and Other Outdoor Sites
- Behind, under, or inside vehicles. Hide behind the engine block or tires to avoid being struck by skipping bullets and shrapnel.
- Inside storage sheds
- Inside or behind portable toilets

Bathroom
If you hear shots outside the bathroom door:

- Stay inside.
- Lock the door if you can.
- Get in a stall, lock the door and crouch on the toilet.
- Stay quiet.

BARRICADES

If time permits, build a barricade as a barrier between you and the threat. If there are two good places to hide, choose the one that allows you to barricade yourself. Determine this now, before violence erupts.

If the assailant is armed with a knife, the barrier needs only to slow or prevent him from getting close enough to cut you. If he

Don't Give Up a Good Hiding Place
There is a tendency with some people to give up a good hiding place when the pressure is on. That is how I caught many hiding suspects during my police career. If they hadn't given up their hiding places when the police were near but unaware of their position, we would have never found them.

Fight the temptation to give up a good hiding place. However, if it's clearly not a good place, move when you have an opportunity and an avenue of escape.

has a firearm, especially a high-powered rifle, you want a barrier that stops penetrating bullets as well as keeps him away from you.

Remember: concealment, such as a stack of empty boxes, hides you but doesn't stop a bullet. Cover hides you and can stop a bullet. Those large, floor-model copy machines that hold reams of paper do a good job of stopping high-powered rounds, as do piles of gym mats, some vending machines, and cafeteria ovens. If these things are positioned in such a way that the shooter can't easily see behind them, squeeze into the space and crouch down.

Jam a door. When you're inside a room where the door swings inward, push desks, file cabinets, and any other heavy furniture against it. Cram items under the door, such as clothing, rulers, erasers, books, anything that will make it difficult to open. An examination of past incidents shows that when a shooter has difficulty gaining entry to a place, he gives up and moves on.

Spend your time behind the barricade looking for a weapon to use against the shooter should he find you. Is there a stapler within reach? A backpack? A track shoe with cleats? A heavy book?

CALLING THE POLICE

Don't assume that someone else has called the police. It's OK if the 9-1-1 emergency center receives more than one call about what is going on. It actually helps them validate the call more quickly; besides, additional callers might have additional information. Tell the 9-1-1 dispatcher that there is an *active shooter* on your campus. The dispatcher and the police will know exactly what that means. Then tell them the name and location of your school. It's common for callers under duress to forget to tell 9-1-1 where the incident is occurring or forget what the numerical address is. Consider noting it in your cell phone directory and posting it by your desk or wall phone.

If you're calling from a wall phone in your classroom or a desk phone in the office and the 9-1-1 dispatcher asks you to stay on the line but doing so might jeopardize your safety, tell the dispatcher that you can't, then drop the phone (but leave the connection open) and run. This allows the dispatcher to hear what is happening. If you're on a cell phone, stay on with the dispatcher so you can continue to update her as to what is going on.

No matter which phone you use, if for some reason you hang up, stay off the phone so the 9-1-1 dispatcher can recontact you if needed. If you do use a cell phone, make sure to leave it turned on. Since you don't want a ringing cell phone to give away your posi-

A Word about Phones

A cell phone doesn't provide the dispatch center with the same complete, automatic, computerized information about who is calling and from where that a landline does. So if you have a choice, use the landline. A cell phone may show the area you're calling from within a block or so, but it's still hit and miss at this point. If you have a landline or use an Internet phone, make sure it's registered with 9-1-1 through the service provider. Otherwise, your call could go as far as another county.

tion, put it on vibrate. Consider always keeping it on vibrate while at school. If yours is still audible in this mode, turn it off. It's quite common for people to want to call their parents or best friend and tell them what is going on, but don't do it. They can't help you; the police can.

It's critical that the police get as much information as possible for their safety and your safety, and for them to be able to approach the scene using the best tactics and strategy.

They will want to know:

- The name of the school and address where the incident is occurring
- The description of the shooter or shooters. It's imperative that the police know how many there are. Without that information, it's difficult for them to contain the area and dangerous for everyone concerned
- If there is more than one shooter
- If there are other armed people on the site: a teacher, a school security officer, the principal. The police might not be able to differentiate between the suspect (especially when it's an adult) and a private citizen brandishing a weapon wanting to help
- Where he is right now: which building, what floor, where on the grounds, where he was last seen, and which direction he was heading
- The layout of the campus or grounds, including entry points for the officers and possible exit points for the shooter
- What kind of weapon he has. Officers approach a suspect armed with a knife differently than one armed with a firearm. Tell the police if you saw a handgun or a high-tech rifle. Did you see any evidence of explosives or extra ammunition?
- Who is he? Does anyone know him? Is he a student?
- How many rounds has he fired?
- Has he made threats to harm others?
- Did you see a vehicle?

- Did he arrive on foot?
- If he was dry even though it's raining out? (Might indicate he arrived in a vehicle.)
- If anyone is hurt?
- Where are the injured?
- How many are injured?
- Has he locked people in?
- Has he taken hostages?
- Has he said anything?
- Is there a known grudge?
- Is he specifically looking for one or more people?
- Is there anyone—staff, security officer, parent—there who has a gun?
- What is happening right now?

HOW THE POLICE SEE IT

After Columbine, where police followed the standard procedure of "buying time" until SWAT arrived, more and more police agencies are training street officers to take immediate action in schools where the suspect(s) is using or has the potential to use, deadly force. Some street officers carry semiautomatic rifles in their trunks as well as ballistic vests and helmets for the purpose of entering a hot zone and ending a situation before additional lives are lost. Many agencies call this "rapid response" or "rapid deployment."

Not all police agencies agree with this, and continue with the strategy of time, talk, and tactics. As a former police officer, I believe that this antiquated thinking is hard to defend. Consider this: If it's you hiding under your desk and draping your body over two trembling children as a deranged kid sprays bullets into screaming students outside your door, do you want police officers to wait 40 minutes out on the street until SWAT arrives?

Police must consider:

1. The shooter's state of mind
- The police are likely dealing with a person who has been pushed to his limit by anything and everything from a troubled home life to school bullies to what he considers unfair treatment by teachers and staff. He has reached his breaking point.
- The shooter might think that everyone has been deliberately making his life miserable and now the police are "interfering" in it too. So he might as well take out as many people as he can, even himself.

2. The shooter's tactical advantage
- The school campus offers more hiding places, entrances, and exits than does the shooter's home.
- There are many places where he might have previously stored weapons and explosives.
- If the shooter has been attending school there for many years, he might feel comfortable on this battleground, much more comfortable than the police.

Obey the Police

Since the police don't know who everyone is when they burst into a scene where kids and teachers have been injured and killed, they are going to treat everyone as suspects until they can determine who's who. They know that sometimes a suspect leaves a hectic crime scene by pretending to be one of the victims. Therefore, should the police yell at you to raise your hands and lie down on your stomach, do so without hesitation.

On one occasion, I nearly shot an armed homeowner at the scene of a burglary in progress. Right after he had called 9-1-1, he got his gun and began searching his home. Three minutes later when I confronted a man with a gun in his hand, I shouted at him to drop the weapon and to get down. The homeowner hesitated for a long moment, a moment in which he continued to hold his gun, a moment in which I was looking at him over my gun barrel, a moment that was nearly his last on Earth.

Obey the police. It will save your life.

OTHER EMERGENCY SERVICES

The police will likely arrive first but other emergency agencies will come, too. The fire department's medical team will respond and, if there is a fire, fire trucks. Ambulances will help with the injured. No matter if there is a large working fire and there are injured in the building and out on the grounds, fire fighters and emergency medical technicians (EMT) will wait outside the perimeter until the police say it's safe for them to come onto the scene. In the event there are explosives involved or the shooter has not been apprehended—he might be on foot in the area or he could be lying injured or lying dead but he hasn't been identified as the shooter—firefighters and EMTs might have to stay away for a considerable time.

"Don't Become Part of the Problem"

This saying among law enforcement refers to everything from officers driving recklessly to an emergency to them dashing fool-ishly into a high-risk situation without backup. The saying also applies to people on the scene of a school shooting, especially when the perpetrator is still loose somewhere in the school. It's imperative that until the situation is contained that emergency per-sonnel, as well as school staff and parents, don't become part of the problem by rushing into a school shooting scenario and getting shot or taken hostage.

When medical people enter the scene, some of their actions might be misinterpreted as they rush about performing triage, roughly defined as the sorting and allocation of treatment to the injured according to the urgency of their need for care. When the shooter isn't known and it's unknown where he is, it's likely that the police will search all of those injured for weapons before they are transported by ambulances. This too might be misinterpreted and cause frustration and anger.

Understand that the police and other emergency units are coming into an incident *after* it's over or *as* it's unfolding. Think of all those times you have been channel surfing and you found a movie that was already in progress. As you watched what was happening at that moment, you simultaneously struggled to piece together what had already happened and who the good and the bad guys were. That can be what it's like for the police and other emergency people who enter a situation that has been playing out for several minutes. But here is the difference. You're playing catch-up in the comfort and safety of your living room. In a real school shooting, emergency crews know that there is a brazen killer still loose on the sprawling campus who might be the same age as, and dressed similarly to, hundreds of other people.

ASSISTING WOUNDED CLASSMATES

You're lying behind a hallway vending machine and you can see Lisa, the girl in your third period, lying on the floor in the hallway. She is moving, but barely, as the pool of blood by her head widens with each passing second. You can hear the shooter ranting somewhere off to your right, and you heard another shot a couple of minutes ago. You can see Lisa, but you don't know if the shooter can see her or the vending machine. You want desperately to scoot out from behind your cover, scurry over to her, and pull her to safety. While there are unknowns as to where the kid with the gun is, you know for certain that Lisa needs help. What do you do?

In any given situation, there are so many variables, large and small, that it's impossible and even unwise to suggest specific techniques in a book. However, here are a few factors to think about before you find yourself in this terrible situation:

Deciding to Move to the Injured Person
* Where is the shooter?
* How far is it between you and the injured person?
* Are there cover and concealment opportunities between the two of you?
* Are you big enough and strong enough for the task?
* Will you have help?
* Where will you drag or carry the injured person?

What about the Shooter?
* Wait until he leaves the immediate area.
* If he has proceeded into another room, consider positioning a lookout at the door to warn you of his return or to attack him with an improvised weapon as he enters.

Moving the Injured
* Drag the injured to cover or concealment as quickly and quietly as possible.
* If the person's injury necessitates careful movement and you have time, move behind his head, cross your arms, reach under his head, and grab the clothing on his shoulders. With his head resting on your crossed forearms, pull him to safety.
* If the person is on his stomach, turn him over as one unit to prevent further injury.
* If you must move the person up or down stairs or for a great distance, carry him on your back with his arms draped over your shoulders and across your chest, his legs trailing behind you. Bring one or two people to help watch for the shooter and to switch off when one of you fatigues.

The decision to leave your place of cover to help an injured classmate when the shooter is still in the area is a judgment call only you can make given the totality of all the variables of the situation. Consider the above points and think about it now.

Don't become part of the problem. Force yourself to wait so that you're alive to take advantage of a better opportunity, one that will save students and teachers lives and keep yours intact.

But . . . is it possible that the opportunity might come too late? Sadly, yes.

An Ugly Reality for Teachers

There is a distinct possibility that you might have to stay crouched behind cover and watch as a student—a child that you have taught, nurtured, reprimanded, guided, and laughed with—dies. Many police officers and soldiers have suffered this experience, and it's important to consider that you could, too.

It's tough to watch a child or another teacher writhe in pain and call out for help; indeed, it's the stuff of lifelong nightmares. But an ongoing, deadly situation might not allow for a rescue without you getting hurt or killed. "Tombstone courage" makes for fascinating war stories, but you might not survive to get your medal.

Chapter 6

Fighting Back

I would have profound gratitude to any teacher who shot an armed student who was trying to shoot my kid or other kids.
—Anonymous parent

Fighting back should be considered a last-ditch response when all other options have been eliminated. Under what circumstances you should or should not fight back needs to be pondered before you're faced with the decision, not after your world has exploded into bloody bedlam. You need to give serious thought as to whether you have what it takes to leap on someone armed with a gun. Or smash someone in the head with a barbell plate from the gym or with a heavy stapler from your desk. Here are a couple of things you need to think about:

Could you seriously injure or kill this person? If you say yes, is your answer coming from deep within you? Or is it just bravado? If you say no, are you willing to live (or die) because of your inaction? See why it's important to think about it now, before violence explodes?

Ask yourself under what circumstances would you fight back? Don't just say "to protect myself or the lives of others." You must be specific. Use your visualization skills to create several realistic scenarios and imagine your response. Develop at least a basic sense of when you would act and when you would wait.

It's important as a parent that you talk to your kids about fighting back. It's not an easy discussion because as you will see in this chapter, there is a host of variables involved. It might even be argued that *how* your child fights back is an easier decision for them than *if* and precisely *when* they should fight back. Here is how the debate looks in simple terms:

- Don't fight back and your child becomes an easy target.
- Do fight back and your child survives and maybe saves the lives of others.
- Do fight back and your child becomes the focus of the shooter.

As you read this chapter, keep in mind the physical and psychological make-up of each of your children. With that understanding, talk to them all together about fighting back and with each one individually. Listen to their thoughts on it and then express yours. Should you hear indications of bravado and Hollywood heroics, address them as unrealistic and dangerous. Emphasize the concept of fighting back as a last resort, using the scenarios and suggestions in this chapter.

High school and middle school children will grasp the material here more easily than younger kids. With the older ones, emphasize the concept of opportunity and weapon choice.

With the younger children, emphasize that they must hide or run, responses covered earlier in this book. But should the bad guy get them, they must fight with all they have: claw, scream, kick, flail, and throw things. Don't just scratch the shooter's face and stop to see his reaction, but go berserk, all out, non-stop. I used to tell my kids when they were little to "go crazy" or "go nuts" on a bad guy who has them. Use whatever verbiage works for your children.

I have taught the martial arts since 1965, thousands of students from five years of age to 72. It never fails to amaze me how everyone, even seemingly meek and mild people, have an inner savage that is capable of "going nuts" on an opponent. While a veteran black belt has greater finesse to her moves and strategy, the newer student, when presented with the right stimulus, is capable of tremendous ferocity. Fear, anger, and the threat of death is such a stimulus. Talk with your children about how to channel that to survive.

WHO SHOULD FIGHT BACK?

Teachers, staff, campus security, visiting adults, and high school students are the most obvious candidates. Several times, quick-thinking adults were able to stop a shooter:

- After a 13-year-old boy shot four classmates in Oklahoma, a science teacher approached the boy, who was still pulling the trigger on his empty gun. He grabbed the boy's arms and pinned him against a brick wall.
- In Moses Lake, Washington, a 14-year-old armed with two pistols shot four people in his class before taking hostages. At one point in the siege, a teacher rushed and tackled him to the floor.
- A 14-year-old boy in Edinboro, Pennsylvania, brought a gun to his graduation dance and opened fire, killing one student and wounding three others. The banquet hall owner, armed with a shotgun, went after the boy, disarmed him, and held him for the police.

There have also been shootings where students subdued a shooter:

- At Thurston High School in Springfield, Oregon, students tackled shooter Kip Kinkel and slammed him to the ground after one of his weapons ran out of ammunition. One of the tacklers was even wounded.

- A 14-year-old student in Paducah, Kentucky, opened fire on a prayer group, killing three and wounding five. The shooting stopped when another student tackled him to the ground.
- In Red Lake, Minnesota, a six-foot, 250-pound middle school kid brought three high-powered guns to school and commenced to kill eight people and wound another seven. Another student, a 15-year-old, 300-pound football player, made the decision not to let him kill any more of his friends in his classroom. He rushed the shooter and tried to stab him with a pencil but a bulletproof vest deflected it. He continued to wrestle with the armed kid until the shooter managed to discharge a round into his face. The hero would survive and be credited for saving the lives of all the students in the room.

Should Grade School Children Be Taught to Fight Back?

A series of recently produced videotapes shows an armed person rushing into a classroom where he is overwhelmed by a throng of students. The video, produced by Texas security experts, teaches kids to throw their books, backpacks, chairs, and desks with the intention of hurting and dominating the shooter. The slant of the tapes teaches kids not to let the predator take control. A spokesperson for the company argues that a dozen or more sixth, seventh, and eighth graders can be an effective force. Swarming the shooter doesn't give him a chance to collect his thoughts, so goes the argument. The kids mob him and strike him with anything and everything.

While one school district in Texas, with 14 schools, supports the program and wants every student trained, other security experts are aghast at the idea. If SWAT teams are not always sure how to approach an active school shooter, they ask, how can young children know what to do? Of course, the dynamics are different in that the kids are on the scene as it erupts while a SWAT team doesn't get there until much later. But perhaps the real point of the question is can young children be expected to know, given all the variables of a horrific moment that is a school shooting, when they should or should not swarm?

The critics also bring up the good point that the one child who leads the rush is most vulnerable to getting shot. The security company agrees, but argues that the risk may be worth it to save lives.

An online poll conducted by ABC News found that out of 161,749 voters, 41 percent thought it was a bad idea, 41 percent thought it was a good idea, and 18 percent were not sure.

Clearly this is open to debate.

Your Survival Is Your Responsibility

While your school district and principal are responsible for providing and maintaining a safe environment for you—which can be as simple as keeping outside access doors locked or as elaborate as uniformed security on the campus, alarm systems, secure areas, and clip-on ID badges—the reality is that the school can't control everything all the time. You need to accept the possibility that you might find yourself in a position where you have to fight back physically. You can wish that it wasn't such a dangerous world and you can try to convince yourself that school shootings only happen elsewhere, but wishing won't change anything. However, being alert, aware, and prepared will.

Being alert and aware is a condition—Condition Yellow—that you function in every day when you leave your home. Being prepared is what you do right now, not next week, not even tomorrow. *Now.* Part of that preparation is the acceptance that, no matter how good the security is at your school, violence can happen anyway. Right in front of you. A kid goes off, or maybe it's a parent, or a teacher's ex-husband or boyfriend. It could even be someone unassociated with the school who found his way through a door. This person has gone over the edge of rage and reason; he is armed and he wants to hurt someone. Kill someone. Kill lots of people.

THE CONFRONTATION

Let's say that at your school there are no security measures in place. Or if there are, they haven't helped because in the midst of the usual morning sounds of kids laughing in the hallway and the clatter of locker doors slamming, several voices shout above the din that "someone's going crazy by the office!"

Let's look at four scenarios and see what you can do in each situation:

1. The attacker is unarmed.
2. The attacker is armed with an improvised weapon.
3. The attacker is armed with a knife.
4. The attacker is armed with a gun.

The Attacker Is Unarmed

A big high school senior has gone berserk. He is kicking and punching walls, screaming, pushing, and hitting anyone who is near. There are many factors to quickly consider:

- His hands are empty, but is he carrying a knife under his jacket or a gun in his waistband?
- Are there environmental weapons—fire ax, trashcan—within his immediate reach?
- How do your size, strength, and physical condition compare to his?

Dog Pile

For our purposes, a dog pile is when two or more people leap on a violent person, knock him to the floor, and restrain him by holding him down with their combined body weight. Think of a football game where several players pile on the man with the ball.

- Are there others nearby who are willing to assist you in controlling him?
- Have you or anyone else notified the principal's office, school security, or the police?
- Would it be better for you to flee?
- Is there an avenue of escape available to you?

If You're Forced to Fight an Unarmed Attacker

You can't get away and there is no avenue of escape; your only option is to fight him:

- You alone or you and a staff member or a student pick up anything within your reach—stapler, paperweight, fire hose, trash can, coffee cup, or whatever else is handy—and throw it at him. When he bends over to cover himself from the onslaught, rush him, take him to the floor, and dog-pile him. Be aggressive here; keep throwing things at him until you have the opening to move in. Accept the fact that you might be the one who has to advance first; others might be hesitant to initiate physical contact.
- Rush him with a chair, desk, large copy machine, table, or any other object of comparable size and weight. Use it to force him to the floor or against a wall and then dog-pile him. It might even be possible to restrain him with the object. Or if someone else distracts him in some way, throw a coat over his head, then force him to the floor and dog-pile him.
- To confuse him, you and three others rush him from his left, right, front, and rear. Knock him to the floor, and dog-pile him.
- Understand that it's likely that you will be punched, clawed, kicked, and bitten as you struggle to subdue him. This is reality—it's a fight, and you must be mentally prepared for it.

The Attacker Is Armed with an Improvised Weapon

The violent person has picked up something from the surroundings: a three-hole punch, dumbbell, PC monitor, or any other object common to your school and potentially injurious. The danger level to you and others is now greater than it was when he was unarmed, so it's important to be aware of your distance from him. Obviously, he can throw a three-hole-punch farther than he can a 30-pound dumbbell. Here are some things to notice:

- Is there an avenue of escape available to you?
- What environmental weapon is within your reach?
- How effective does he seem with the object in his hands? Is he threatening with a large, cumbersome trash can or a more easily wielded and sharp adhesive-tape dispenser?
- When he swings the object, does he maintain his balance or does he stumble or fall?
- Is he right- or left-handed?
- Are you facing him alone or with others willing to deal with him physically?

If You're Forced to Fight an Attacker Armed with an Improvised Weapon

As noted earlier, when you have no choice but to fight, you must do so with total commitment:

- You alone or you and another person need to pick up anything you can to throw.
- Don't try to hit small body parts like his head or his hands; target his mass—his chest and back. Hitting these areas distracts him, possibly hurts him, thus buying you time to flee or rush him. Should you inadvertently hit his vulnerable head or fragile hands, targets that cause excruciating and distracting pain, that's okay. When he is thinking about his pain, he isn't thinking about you. Just don't aim specifically at them.

- If being struck by the thrown object causes him to run out the door to, say, the parking lot, let him go.
- If there is a possibility that he could return, you and the others should run in the opposite direction and/or lock the door behind him.
- If he flees into another part of the school where he might hurt others, and you are physically capable and/or have capable help, pursue him as you continue to throw environmental objects at him. Knock him down and dog-pile him.
- If being struck by your thrown objects forces him to drop his, follow any of the suggestions in the "When he is unarmed" section: Rush him with a trash can, table, or chair, and knock him to the floor with it. Then dog-pile him.
- You and several others surround him to divide his attention. One of you throws a covering over his head—coat, blanket, tarp, or something similar—then rush him, take him to the floor, and dog-pile him.

In regard to timing, the best moments to rush in are when the attacker loses his balance while swinging the object; when he drops the object; throws the object, or swings the object across his body (i.e., say he is right-handed and he swings a stool from right to left. Rush him immediately after he completes his swing, and pin his arm and stool against his chest).

If he is still holding the weapon after you have taken him to the floor, you can dog-pile him, stomp on his arm and hand until he releases it, or grab a finger on the weapon hand and yank it toward the back of his hand until the sprain or break causes him to release the weapon.

The Attacker Is Armed with a Knife

It's been my experience as a police officer that most attackers aren't skilled blade fighters. Still, their victims suffered, some fatally. Unfortunately, many martial arts instructors say to their students, "A real knife fighter will never attack like this (insert any technique)."

Oh really? Can the speaker see into the future?

Though the instructor is referring to a trained person when he says "a *real* knife fighter," if someone is attacking you with a knife, it's real. Most of the knife-wielding attackers I dealt with were mentally deranged, drunk, enraged, or all three. That made them real and deadly, though not one of them had trained formally in martial arts knife fighting. Don't think that Carrie, the overweight girl who perpetually sits in detention, and Rickie, the skinny senior who giggles incessantly, are any less of a threat because of their unassuming physicality. A knife, coupled with an out-of-control mental state, makes anyone a potential killer.

In Longmont, Colorado, a 14-year-old boy, a new ninth grader at Silver Creek High School, stabbed a 14-year-old girl seven times in the back with a pair of scissors for no apparent reason. He then threw the scissors against a wall, where they stuck. He fled downstairs but was quickly arrested by a school resource officer.

The dangers of facing an attacker with a knife are similar to those you'll encounter against a person armed with an improvised weapon. Make note of these important details:

- Is there an avenue of escape available to you?
- If he slashes the air with the knife, does he maintain his balance or does he stumble or fall?
- Are you facing him alone or with others also willing to deal with him physically?
- Has security or the police been notified?

If You're Forced to Fight an Attacker Armed with a Knife
If your only option is to fight, you must move quickly:

- Grab an environmental weapon within your reach: back-pack, ream of paper, baseball bat, cleated track shoe, three-hole punch.
- Keep large environmental objects—desks, copy machines, partitions, chairs, cafeteria serving cart—between you and the threat to slow him down and give you time to plan and react.
- Use a chair to keep the perpetrator from getting within stabbing distance by grasping it with two hands, pointing the legs at him, and blocking his knife thrusts and slashes.
- Grab anything within your reach to throw at him.
- Wrap a coat, tarp, or blanket around your arm. Should you get cornered, feed him your wrapped arm and strike him with your other fist or an environmental weapon.
- Grab his weapon arm and don't let go, even if he flings you

Warning: Don't Get Into Legal Trouble
Some self-defense instructors teach students to stab or cut the assailant after taking the knife from him. If you have been taught to do this—don't do it. Yes, he tried to stab you and others, but once you have taken the blade away, he is no longer an armed, deadly threat. Therefore, you don't have a right to cut or stab him, no matter how angry or frightened you are.

Secure the knife, hand it off to someone, or throw it where the threat can't readily get it: behind a filing cabinet, under a desk, or down a vent. Then wrestle him to the floor and dog-pile him. Historically, many school shooters carry more than one weapon. Therefore, strive to control his hands and arms so that he is unable to access his pockets or waistband, common areas where weapons are carried.

about. Use your body weight to pin his arm against his chest, your side, a wall, the floor, or any other object.

- When the moment is right—a moment only you can determine—release one of your hands and strike a vital target. (See the section entitled, "Hit vital targets" on page 130.)
- If you get cut, keep fighting! If you stop to look at your wound, he will likely cut you again.
- Once you get control of his weapon arm, take him to the floor and dog-pile him.

As soon as he releases his grip on the knife, grab it and toss it behind something, or hand it to someone.

The Attacker is Armed with a Gun

Never make assumptions about someone armed with a handgun on your campus. You might think you know Tommy from math class, but until now did you know he was capable of bringing a weapon to school to hurt and kill people? Do you know if he is going to shoot one person or mow down everyone else in the library? Even if his initial intention is to kill one specific person, do you know if he just might snap even further and shoot someone else, and then another, and another . . . It's happened before in other schools and those people didn't know the shooter was capable of such carnage.

The only absolute, the only thing you know for sure, is that Tommy has a gun in the hallway and he has gone quite mad.

When facing a firearm, there are many serious considerations:

- You hear the shot(s). Was it fired in the same room you're in? An adjoining room? The next building over? One floor down or one floor up? Understand this: You can't always tell from what direction shots are coming. Many times, you aren't even sure if it's shots that you heard.
- Do you have an avenue of escape? You know the answer

because you have studied the area and imagined your response in such an incident.

- Call 9-1-1 while you're moving to or have already reached a safe place. You can do this because you carry a cell phone and you have practiced tapping in 9-1-1, a task that can be difficult under extreme stress. Call even if you think someone else has.
- If there isn't a way out or enough time to get out, is there a place to hide? You know there is because you have looked for it beforehand and imagined how you would hide.
- Are you prepared to fight the gunman when all other options are gone?

You Don't Know His Mind

All the years I was a cop, especially when I worked with street gangs, there were always well-meaning citizens who would say that all a troubled child needs is a warm hug, a smile, and understanding. I recall one woman who came to the gang unit with a plan to solve all the drive-by shootings: Poetry. "We get the disenfranchised youth," she said, after admonishing us for calling them gangbangers, "to write poems about their lives." Her thought was that that would be a way for them to air out their anger.

A young person, or an adult for that matter, who brings a weapon to school, is in a mind-set that is far beyond all the other kids who simply don't like school or don't like other students. A student armed with multiple weapons is in a place mentally—maybe he has been there for several days prior or maybe he just snapped this morning—where he wants to rain down death and destruction.

He doesn't want to write a poem, he doesn't want a hug. And your "understanding" smile? Well, it's just going to give him a target.

If You're Forced to Fight an Attacker Armed with a Gun

Do whatever he says. Don't antagonize him, but be ever watchful for a window of opportunity, one that is open enough to allow you time to cross the space between you and the attacker and grab his weapon. Lift your hands no higher than the barrel and lean your body forward, but not so much that he notices. You can grab faster when your hands are on a straight line to the weapon, and you can lunge faster when your body weight is already leaning forward slightly.

The instant he is distracted, he points the gun away from you, or you feel you have no other option, lunge with all the speed you can muster from your leg muscles, with your arms outstretched to grab the barrel and your upper body turned a little to present a smaller target.

You're hiding behind a large file cabinet when a kid with a rifle passes by, unaware that you're only inches away from him as he stalks the office. Should you give up your hiding place and attack him?

It's a tough decision, one that only you can make given all the information you have at that precise moment. For example, is he looking in the opposite direction from where you're hiding? Is his firearm pointed away from you? Is the path from your hiding spot to him unobstructed? Do you believe he is going to shoot others?

Once you make the decision to move, you must burst from your hiding place like a rocket. You cannot hesitate! You cannot have second thoughts halfway there. Your only objective is to cross that space and grab hold of his weapon.

When grabbing the attacker's weapon arm or the weapon itself, grab with both hands, then ram him with your shoulder; drive him into a wall, against a desk, or into a locker—and hold on. Even if he drives you back into a wall or over chairs, hold on. Gripping his weapon arm or the weapon is a strong position because you can apply all of your arm and body strength against his one arm. Press yourself into him for maximum strength and tuck your head into his chest, his side, or his abdomen to decrease the impact he can deliver. Since he most likely will hit you, expect to eat some pain as you continue to hold on, and hold on you must. During the struggle, always know where the muzzle of the gun is pointing. You don't want it pointing at any part of your body.

When you have a solid grip on a suspect's weapon arm, don't give it up until you have a window of opportunity to take the struggle to the next level, such as a restraint hold, a debilitating blow, or a fast and sure escape. How long? Only you can decide when the moment is right to let go and try something else, such as when :

- the shooter weakens with fatigue or injury;
- you maneuver into a position where you dominate;
- the shooter tries to transition to a different technique;
- you get assistance from one or more classmates or teachers;
- you're about to get shot anyway. Example: You're losing the struggle and the gun barrel is slowly turning toward your head or body mass. If you can't push him or trip him, consider releasing one of your hands and ramming your fingers into his eyes or punching the front of his throat. (What if you are struck by a bullet? See "You've Been Shot" on page 119.)

Handgun-Specific Considerations
If you must fight, you have many factors to consider:

- He will usually (but not always) be closer to you than if he were armed with a rifle.
- He will probably (but not always) hold the gun in one hand and stretch his arm all the way out toward you.
- It's more awkward for him to move his gun arm to the outside of his body than it is to move it across his body. (Therefore, try to approach on the backhand side of his arm.)
- You can only push the barrel right or left when the gun is pointing at your stomach or chest, because to push it up or down means your body will still be in its path. But when the barrel is

pointed at your head, you can push it right, left, or knock it upward a few inches until you are out of the bullet's path.
- He will probably have his finger on the trigger.

Rifle- and Shotgun-Specific Considerations
The mechanics of wielding a long gun are different than the stances used in firing handguns:

- He is more formidable at a distance.
- A rifle is more accurate than a handgun.
- It might be awkward for him to wield a long weapon.
- Notice if he seems comfortable handling the rifle.
- For you to be in hands-on fighting range, you may have to be taken hostage; leap out at him from hiding; or confront him accidentally, such as running into him, literally or figuratively, as you round a corner.

Before attacking a shooter with a rifle or shotgun, hold your hands up about head high, one hand closer to him than the other. As you talk, move them a little so they are in continuous motion and less obvious when you make your move. Remember that it's more awkward for the shooter to swing the rifle to the outside of his body than it is to move it across his body. Therefore, try to approach on the backhand side of his trigger hand.

Once you're in touching range, the elements are similar to fighting a shooter armed with a handgun.

METHODS OF ATTACKING

In the Paladin Press book *The Citizen's Guide to Stopping Suicide Attackers,* author Itay Gil recommends that as the shooter holds his gun on you, raise your hands and cower, lowering your body and head to the height of his gun barrel. To the person holding the gun, this appears to be a natural fear response. While cowering might not take that much acting, the position is a good one tactically. When the moment is right—the shooter is talking, listening to you talk, or is somehow distracted—grab the barrel with one or both hands as fast as you can and jam it upward.

Simultaneously, drive your body weight into him and knock him back or into a hard object.

Hold onto the gun barrel with all your strength. If you're able, ram him with your shoulders, hips, or knees. Bite his neck or face, slam your forehead into his nose, and slam his gun arm into anything hard. Fight with ferocity, and keep that gun barrel pointed up. Keep fighting until you get help or you have weakened him to the point where you can take possession of the weapon.

When headbutting, strike with that part of your head—front, sides, and back—that is covered when wearing a sweatband. Slam your head into the shooter's nose, cheekbone, and temple.

When using this cowering technique, wait until the shooter is talking, when he is listening to you talk, or when he is distracted, then lunge into him as you simultaneously jam the barrel up, down, or to the side with one or both of your hands. If for whatever reason the cowering approach isn't doable for you, choose the right moment, as noted in the previous lists, to grab the barrel and push it away from you as you simultaneously pivot your body out of the line of a bullet's trajectory.

Grab the weapon as the shooter is talking or as he is listening to you or someone else talk. This provides you with an extra fraction of a second as his brain makes the transition from processing language to reacting to your grab.

Whatever technique you use to grab the barrel, maintain a death grip on it as you struggle, keeping it away from you and directed at the floor, up in the air, or to the side. Expect him to pull the gun away from you. Don't resist his pull and turn the moment into a muscle contest, but rather follow the momentum and push your weight into him. Use the strength of your legs to drive him into a wall, door, anything hard. If you're stable enough to knee him, smash him in his groin and take the gun away from him. If you can free one hand, strike any of the vital targets discussed later in "Hit Vital Targets," and do so repeatedly and with extreme prejudice.

RESIST BEING MOVED TO ANOTHER LOCATION

Should the armed subject indicate that he wants you to go to another location, obey him at first while thinking quickly how to attack him or escape. As he follows you with the weapon trained on your back, think offense. In his book, Itay Gil suggests that you slow your pace, even fake a stumble, so the shooter closes in on you close enough for you to reach him. He might even force you with a nudge of the barrel. That is the instant you spin, knock the barrel aside, grab it, and follow up as already suggested. Dangerous? Yes. But so is going willingly to another location, the place where you might be shot.

When you take the weapon away, hit him with it. Butt-stroke him, rake the barrel down his face, or use both hands—one on the barrel and one on or near the stock—to thrust the gnarly middle section into his throat or face.

If you're familiar with how the weapon functions, consider threatening the shooter with it. But you'd better be ready to shoot him, repeatedly if necessary, if he presses his attack. You don't want him taking it back. If you don't know how it works, you're better off hitting him with it and running off. Remember, he might be armed with multiple weapons. Don't stick around to find out.

Get rid of the weapon as soon as you're out of sight of the shooter. Drop it behind a bookcase, file cabinet, or into a trashcan. If you're confronted by the police while you still have it, do exactly as they say—and do so slowly—because they might think you're the shooter. Don't argue that you took it away from him. If they tell you to drop the gun, do so. If they tell you to get down onto your knees or to lie down on the floor, do so. You can explain everything later.

YOU'VE BEEN SHOT

You're struggling with the gunman, the weapon explodes, and a bullet rips through your arm, your belly, or your thigh. You're going to die, right? No. NO! You're not going to die, you're going to continue to fight back. Maybe even harder.

Men and women in today's modern military and law enforcement learn to reach inside themselves to draw out the will to continue to fight, no matter how injured and debilitated they might be. Don't give the assailant the opportunity to strike again. If you are shot while on the run, don't stop. Keep moving to safety. If you're shot in the midst of a struggle, keep fighting.

Tell yourself now that there is no way you're going to give up should you be injured during the course of a fight with someone armed with a weapon in your school. Whether you're shot, knifed, beaten with fists, or struck with an object, you're going to continue to fight back and do so with ferocity. Tell yourself, "OK, he got me once, but he unleashed a ferocious beast." It doesn't matter if you're a couch potato, that you walk with a cane, or that you're convinced you don't have a physical bone in your body. Tell yourself right now that no matter how injured you are, you're going to fight hard and never—never—give up. Do it for your family, do it for your friends, and do it for you.

This is known as a proper combat mind-set, and we will explore this absolutely vital concept next.

YOUR MIND-SET

An untrained person with a powerful, determined, and fierce mind-set is often just as dangerous as someone who has trained in a fighting discipline. I saw this repeatedly during my 29 years in law enforcement, many times having the unfortunate experience of having to physically deal with such people. It doesn't matter that you're not a physical person and as mild mannered as they come. When forced to fight back against a violent person on your campus, you must have a determined mind-set that you're going to survive and you will do whatever is necessary to accomplish that. If

Don't Believe TV and Movies

Movies and television "teach" us that when someone gets shot or stabbed, they die. But that's not the case in real life. The vast majority of gunshot and stabbing victims I saw in my police job survived and even fought back. A small number were unaware of their wounds. Two extreme cases include one man who discovered a hole in his earlobe hours after he had heard a gunshot in a park. (He was intoxicated at the time of the shooting.) The other incident involved a man whose wife had cleanly sliced off his ear with a knife in a family fight. He didn't even know it until I pointed it out to him where it lay under a parked car. I know of two people, a man and a woman, who in separate incidents survived five gunshots to their heads—five!—and one of them was still running around when the police arrived.

Yes, on television and in the movies, "shot" actors fall and don't get up. But in reality, most gunshot wounds are survivable and often the victim continues to function at the scene. When I was shot in the shin, I didn't realize it for several seconds and even then I continued to move about for an hour afterward.

you are hit, stabbed, shot, or run over, so be it, but that cannot deter you from defeating the threat that is trying to hurt or kill you. Your immediate objective is to fight with unbridled ferocity and continue to do so until the threat is no longer present. As is the case with so many other aspects of preparing to survive a school shooting, you must think about this before the incident.

When you have no choice but to fight, know in your mind that without a doubt you are prepared:

- If possible, you'll choose the moment to attack.
- You'll explode on the shooter like a person possessed.
- Your ferocity will put the shooter on the defensive.
- If you get injured, you'll keep fighting.
- You'll reach into that part of your brain that remains primal and interested only in your preservation, bring it forth, and unleash its force.
- You're fighting for yourself, your family, and the students and teachers at your school.
- You'll stop the shooter!
- If forced to, you'll kill him!

The Power of Words

The trend today is to soften reality with a euphemism: a blood-thirsty gangbanger is a "disenfranchised youth;" a political candidate who steals from the campaign contribution fund says he "made a mistake." Because the thought of killing someone in self-defense isn't a pleasant one, many people attempt to soften it with vague terminology. "I'll drop the guy," they say. Or, "I'll do him." "Terminate him." "Take him out." "Waste him."

While these words are arguably more palatable to the mind, police and military trainers say that there is an inherent risk attached to their use. If it's distasteful for you to think kill and to say kill, it's quite possible that your actions, which are directed by your mind, will be insufficient for the needs of the situation. An action intended only to "drop" the shooter or simply "do him" just might allow him to continue to hurt and kill people.

If the shooter is trying to kill you, has already killed, or is trying to kill others, and you have no avenue of escape and no other options, then killing him is what needs to be done. Think about this and prepare yourself for the possibility.

Mental Imagery

As boxers, wrestlers, martial artists, soldiers, and law enforcement officers know, mental imagery is a powerful training method for preparing to fight back. Follow the relaxation procedure as described in Chapter 4 and then see yourself confronting someone armed with a weapon who is trying to hurt you or someone else.

Begin by visualizing a physically violent unarmed person con-

Commitment

You have gone to school with the kid since first grade. Or as a teacher, you have worked hard with the student because you recognized his potential and that he was troubled in some way. However, the violent, out-of-control person in front of you now isn't that same person. Something has pushed him over the edge, a place where he is deliberately hurting everyone in his path.

That harsh reality must be in the forefront of your mind to guide your actions. Since there is no other option than to deal with him on a physical level, you must go into the confrontation with a powerful commitment to neutralize him. Your immediate objective is to take him down hard and fast, and then restrain him by using the combined body weight of as many people as it takes.

Once he is restrained and no longer able to hurt people, call the police and then you can try to talk him into calming down.

fronting you, say, in a hallway. After you have practiced that scenario for three or four separate sessions, visualize confronting a person armed with an object from your school—a three-hole punch, for example, or a baseball bat. After three or four sessions of this, graduate to confronting a person armed with a knife. Lastly, visualize dealing with a person with a firearm.

It's impossible to visualize every variation of a confrontation, but by investing five minutes once a day for a couple of weeks, you will make the possibility of an incident real in your mind, and you'll have a sense of what you need to do if violence comes calling.

Review the previous sections on the elements of confronting an unarmed and armed person in this chapter and incorporate them into your mental imagery practice. Here are the basics:

- Choose a location in your school to visualize the confrontation.
- *See* the person standing a few feet from you, armed or unarmed.
- *See* and *feel* yourself seize a window of opportunity to rush him.
- *See* and *feel* your hands strike his eyes, his throat, and his nose.
- *See* and *feel* your hands and body force him to the floor.
- *See* and *feel* your body drape on him and pin him to the floor.

WEAPONS EVERYWHERE

No matter where you are in your school, keep in mind that you're always in the midst of a weapons cache. But to know it exists, you have to see all the objects as being used for more than their intended purpose. The following is only a partial list of ordinary items in your school to use as weapons to defend your life.

Weapons in the Classroom
- Stapler: Strike the attacker's face, throat, weapon hand, and groin.
- Pen/pencil: Jab, stab, and scrape his face.

- 500-sheet ream of copy paper: Grab it with both hands as if it were a large stone and slam it down onto his head.
- Coffee cup: Throw the hot liquid into his face or use the cup to slam his head, weapon hand, and groin.
- Scissors: Stab him anywhere.
- Telephone receiver: Strike his face, throat, groin, and weapon hand.
- Heavy book: Grab it with both hands and slam it into his head. Use the corner of a paperback to jab his eye, throat, and groin.
- Chair: Hit him with it and when he is on the floor, slam it on top of him and use it to hold him down.
- Heavy flower pot: Throw it at him.
- Fire extinguisher: Spray his face and then hit him with the canister.

Weapons in the Faculty Room

- Coffee pot and mugs: Throw the hot liquid into the attacker's face and use the cup to slam his head, weapon hand, and groin.
- Knives and forks: Stab his body or scrape or slice his face.
- Hot soup: Throw into his face.
- Cleaning liquids (e.g., ammonia) under the sink: Splash into his face.
- Books and magazines: Strike his face, throat, or groin with the corner of the book. Roll the magazine into a tight tube and use it to strike or jab his face and throat.

Weapons in the Custodian's Room

- Heavy tool: Hit the attacker anywhere with it.
- Heavy box: Use it to block a knife attack, to throw at the threat, and to slam on top of him when he is down.
- Fire extinguisher: Spray him in the face and then hit him with the canister.
- Dangerous liquid chemicals: Throw or spray them in his face.

- Water cooler jug: Throw it at the attacker or use it to hold him down.
- Barrel or large box: Throw it at him or use it to hold him down.
- Mop: Throw it at the attacker or strike him with it.

Weapons in the Gym
- Balls: Throw at the attacker.
- Trash can lid: Use it to block and strike.
- Hockey sticks: Use them to block and strike.
- Barbell plates: Throw.
- Wrestling mats: Drape over the attacker and pin him to the floor.

Weapons in the Cafeteria
- Chair or stool: Block with or strike.
- Serving tray: Block with or strike.
- Dishes: Throw at the subject.
- Boiling water: Throw onto the subject.
- Utensils: Strike with or stab.
- Trash can lid: Blocking and striking.
- Table: Ram into the subject.

A Fight Is an Ugly Thing
A fight of any intensity is an ugly thing, more so when it's a desperate match against an armed person. Thinking, "Oh, he doesn't really want to hurt anyone" is dangerously naïve and might very well be the last opinion you ever hold. When a student brings a weapon to school and begins to use it, that person is no longer your classmate. He is a deadly force that might very well take you from your loved ones.

Every person has within them a warrior spirit. When you have no other choice, you must reach deep inside yourself for yours and unleash it to fight with fierce determination for your safety and the safety of others.

Weapons in the Parking Lot

- Objects on your person: Keys for stabbing and scraping, backpack for blocking and striking, umbrella for jabbing, lunch box for blocking and striking, heavy coffee container for striking.
- Parking lot gravel and stones: Gravel for throwing at a distance and stones for hitting at close range.
- Trash can lid: For blocking with and striking.
- Cones or barricades: Cones for throwing at him and barricades to slam him with.

War story: A policeman friend once confronted a burglar who had just climbed over a wall and dropped down next to a garage door a few feet from where the officer sat in his car. Uncommon for a burglar, the man was 6 feet, 6 inches tall, with a massive chest and huge arms. The small officer decided there was no way he was going to get out of his car and physically deal with this monster, so he took advantage of the burglar's hemmed-in position and inched his car forward, pinning him painlessly between the garage door and car's push bumper. Then he waited for backup officers.

Now that is a good example of using a convenient object as a weapon!

Virtually every object around you in your school is a weapon to distract, debilitate, hurt, and even to kill a person who is trying to hurt or kill you.

Do this for one week: Every time you have a spare minute, just 60 seconds, choose one object within your grasp and ask yourself this: How many ways could I use this thing to defend myself? Do this four times a day with four different objects for one week and by Friday afternoon, you'll have added 20 weapons to your arsenal as well as new knowledge and confidence.

Newport Bay - Vancouver Plaza
7717 NE Vancouver Plaza Dr
Vancouver
(360) 896-9795

Card#: **570651**

RUI Card

You have the following reward:

Dining Credits   10.00

You have accrued the following
points toward your next reward:

Points   0
Dollars Spent   0.00

THE FIGHT: DISSECTED

As long as the threat has hold of the weapon—whether it's a stapler, knife, or firearm—he is dangerous and you and everyone else are at risk. If he continues to grip his weapon as you slam him into walls, as you both fall over chairs and crash to the floor, you must take his arm and hand out of the equation.

Pinning the Shooter to the Floor
Pinning a violent person on the floor isn't about strength but about knowing how. Here are critical elements that increase your chances of success:

- Get him onto his stomach to decrease his mobility and his ability to punch and kick.
- You kneel on one side of him as another person kneels on the other.
- Force his arms straight out from his sides in a crucifixion pose, palms up (his palms must face up to lock his elbows, which makes it difficult for him to bend his arms).
- Place one hand on his elbow and the other on his wrist as your partner does the same on the other side. Lean your weight onto the two points, especially his elbow, the primary leverage point.
- A third helper should lie across his knees.
- Hold him in this position until additional help arrives.

Should the person tolerate the pain and begin to defeat the hold, use the heel side of your fist to strike down hard and repeatedly onto his upper arm, forearm, wrist, and hand. These blows are especially painful to the shooter when the floor supports his arm. Should his weapon be one that is especially lethal, such as a cutting instrument or firearm, strike the back of his head and neck area to stun him and maybe even knock him unconscious. This is a vulnerable part of his skull, even more so when the floor supports his head. Know that this is a potentially lethal target, so be sure you're justified before you resort to it.

When You're Alone

Never has the hallway felt so empty on a school day as it does right now as you stand face to face with a teen holding a handgun. You can feel your every heartbeat in your throat as you look into his crazed yet frighteningly calm eyes. Then he looks off to the side. Because you have thought about this moment and imagined what you would do, you seize it, and lunge forward and grab him in an arms-pinned bear hug. But he still has the weapon and he still has enough wrist mobility to shoot you. If he were holding a knife, he could cut you. If he were gripping a three-hole punch, he could still move his hand enough to smack you in the knee or groin.

Once you have a hold on him, you must neutralize that arm and hand.

Draw on all the strength you can muster to slam his weapon arm into something hard: desk, doorframe, wall, or trophy case. Knobs, sharp corners, and edges are especially painful. Don't stop after he weakens and drops the weapon; keep on smashing him until he weakens enough for you to take him to the floor, preferably on his stomach. Be careful not to position him within reach of his dropped weapon. Lie across his upper back and neck, and pin his arms to the floor. Push down on his elbow joint for a leverage advantage.

Should he try to push himself up with his hands or reach for the dropped weapon or something else to use, smash the heel side of your fist against the back of his hand, his fingers, the large forearm muscle near his elbow, or the back of his head. You can hit one of these targets repeatedly, two of them repeatedly, or hit all of them one after the other until he stops trying to get up or reach the weapon. The order in which you hit them depends on what targets he gives you. Hit the one closest first. Continue to lie on top of him, hitting him whenever necessary, until help arrives.

Grab a finger and jerk it in the direction it isn't supposed to go, and break it. This is acutely painful and forces the subject's mind to focus on the intense agony radiating from his injury, and not on you.

When You've Got Help

You and two other people are standing face-to-face with the armed subject. When the moment is right, the three of you rush him, preferably from three angles: his front, his right, and his left. Whoever has the weapon side must secure that arm and never let it go. Grab his elbow and his wrist or hand, and jam his arm forcefully down and against his body. Pin the weapon against his person and keep pushing it against him no matter how you get knocked around as you and your helpers wrestle him to the floor. If it's a firearm, fight with all that you have to keep the barrel pointed down. If, because of his superior strength or some other reason, you cannot pin his arm to his body, hold onto it no matter how he pulls and pushes, and ride it all the way down. Hold his arm against the floor—you have the most leverage when you push in the area of his elbow—using as much of your body weight as possible.

Hit him hard and hit him often! When the moment is right for

Fighting a "Friend"

It's frightening and not just a little bizarre to think that you just might have to fight a student you have taught or, if you're a student, fight a friend you have gone to school with, to save your life or the life of another. It's happened before on school campuses, and it's a safe assumption to think that none of those people who suddenly had to defend themselves ever thought they would be in such a position either. But by reading this book, thinking about it, planning for it, and imagining it, you're far more prepared than most of those who have faced such a critical moment before.

you to release one hand, strike him in any of his vital targets: eyes, ears, nose, and throat. If your classmates are already doing that, then you should hammer on his weapon arm: punch the back of his hand, his wrist bones, the tender muscle on top of his forearm next to his elbow, and the tender belly of his biceps. Grab a finger and bend it back until he releases the weapon. (Be prepared for it to break with an audible snap. Now isn't the time to get squeamish.) If he tolerates the pain and doesn't release the weapon, keep hitting. If he starts to free his arm, stop the hitting and return to holding onto him with two hands. Communicate to your partners what is happening so that one or both of them can strike at his vital targets.

When he finally releases his hold on the weapon, don't let go of him. Whoever can free a hand should grab the weapon and throw it across the room or toss it behind anything that makes it hard for the shooter to retrieve it should he get free. If there is another person there, hand it to him. Dog-pile the shooter and wait for the police.

Hit Vital Targets

You want to strike targets that debilitate quickly—eyes, neck, nose, ears, groin, and fingers—in that order. These targets don't require great skill to hit, or great impact to do damage. There just needs to be an opportunity to reach them.

Eyes: Use your fingers or an environmental weapon to gouge, dig, flick, and scrape.
Effect: Excruciating pain, heavy tearing and blurring, partial blindness (permanent blindness is rare but possible).

Neck: Use your fist, side of your hand, foot, or an environmental weapon to hammer his throat, the sides of his neck, or the back of his neck.
Effect: Blows to the front of the neck cause excruciating pain

and a sensation of choking. A hard blow to the sides or back of the neck causes extreme pain, confusion, and loss of coordination.

Nose: Use your fist, palm, heel, foot, or an environmental weapon to strike.
Effect: Extreme pain, tearing of the eyes, and mental confusion.

Ears: Use your fist, palm, heel, foot, or environmental weapon to strike.
Effect: Extreme pain, a powerful sense of an implosion within the head, and confusion.

Groin: Use any part of your body or environmental weapon to strike, rip, and squeeze.
Effect: Extreme pain and nausea.
Note: While self-defense classes often emphasize kicking and punching the groin, impact to this target doesn't have an effect on everyone. It's recommended that you strike the groin multiple times and/or follow with blows to any of the other vulnerable targets listed here.

Fingers: Use your fist, heel, foot, or an environmental weapon to strike, crush, and break. Use your hand to grab a finger and break it by jerking it across the back of the threat's hand.
Effect: Excruciating pain and possible debilitation of the entire arm.

Don't depend on one blow to do the job. Many people in an agitated mental state are impervious to pain. Plan right now to strike these targets repeatedly until the shooter weakens, drops to the ground, or gives up.

For easy-to-learn instruction on this topic, check out my video *Vital Targets: A Street-Savvy Guide to Targeting the Eyes, Ears, Nose, and Throat,* available from Paladin Press.

Same Attack, Different Effect

Consider the different effect the same technique has when delivered to two different types of targets.

- A hard punch to the shooter's shoulder or a hard punch to the fine bones on the back of his hand
- An index-finger jab into his stomach or an index-finger jab into his eye socket
- A stomp onto a downed shooter's chest or a stomp onto his Adam's apple

While a blow to the first target in each of these comparisons hurts, the same blow delivered to the second one is not only more acute, it's more debilitating and demoralizing. In other words, you get two effects for the price of one blow.

Aim for:

- Eyes, ears, nose, throat, and groin
- Elbows and knees
- Fingers and toes
- Bones in the back of his hand
- Bones in the top of his foot

Conclusion

The art of war teaches us to rely not on the likelihood of the enemy's not coming, but on our own readiness to receive him; not on the chance of his not attacking, but rather on the fact that we have made our position unassailable.

—Sun Tzu

A school shooter walks casually through the halls firing at anyone who crosses his path. There is awful screaming, desperate shouting, and terrible panic. It's over for those who die, but for some of the survivors, those wounded physically and psychologically, there will be a lifetime of mental trauma. "We were so helpless," they say. "What could we have done?"

Police officers and soldiers train continuously to function in such mayhem, using high-tech weaponry and sophisticated methods of combat. But how do teachers and older students prepare for such horror? How do parents prepare their very young children?

First, you must accept that school shootings are happening seemingly more than ever before and there is no way to predict where one will happen next. Then you prepare for it using every means available to you:

- You talk about it with parents, teachers, police, and staff.
- You study your school tactically.
- You trust your gut instinct about people. You monitor that per-

son who has been demonstrating mood swings, making threats, or just acting strangely.

- You ask yourself "what if" questions: "What would I do if a shooter came in that door?" "What if he came down that hall?" "What if he came into the cafeteria?"
- You practice mental imagery. It's the next best thing to physical practice to prepare you for the real thing.
- You tell yourself that if you have no option but to fight, you're going to attack like a person possessed.

You can survive with the information contained in this book and the right mind-set. Decide right now that you won't be a victim; you won't be a sheep led to slaughter. Should violence erupt in your school, you'll instantly begin thinking strategically, defensively, and offensively. You'll go home at the end of the day to your loved ones because *there isn't anything that is going to stop you.*
Prepare now.

About the Author

Loren Christensen and Rocky.

Loren W. Christensen is a Vietnam veteran, a retired police officer with 29 years of law enforcement experience, and a martial artist since 1965. His police experience includes working gang enforcement, street patrol, dignitary protection, and three years spent teaching in several middle schools on a variety of topics of concern to kids.

As a writer, Loren has penned 40 books and dozens of magazine articles on a variety of subjects. While his target audience is most often what he calls "the warrior community"—martial artists, cops, and soldiers—his writing, which includes a variety of other subjects, is also popular among high school and college students, parents, and professionals of every kind.

He can be contacted through his website at www.lwcbooks.com.